THE ART OF PRESERVING WEALTH

MARIO V. SICARI

A GUIDE FOR PRE & POST RETIREES AND BABY BOOMERS

THE ART OF PRESERVING WEALTH

A Guide for Pre & Post Retirees and Baby Boomers

eBook: ISBN 978-1-949513-54-7

Paperback: ISBN 978-1-949513-55-4

Published by DP Group LLC

This book is dedicated to the countless people who have achieved financial success through hard work and sacrifice.

It is dedicated to the colleagues and numerous clients I have mentored in basic financial principles.

Finally, it is dedicated to my staff, my family, and the people who have allowed me to be even a small part of their success.

GET IN TOUCH

Mario.sicari@bgs-fg.com

TABLE OF CONTENTS

INTRODUCTION

The current growth of the population ages 65 and older, driven by the large baby boom generation—those born between 1946 and 1964 — is unprecedented in U.S. history.

This aging of the U.S. population has brought both challenges and opportunities to the economy, infrastructure, and institutions.

The number of Americans ages 65 and older is projected to increase from 58 million in 2022 to 82 million by 2050 (a 41% increase), and the 65-and-older age group's share of the total population is projected to rise from 17% to 23%.[1]

Education levels are increasing. Among people aged 65 and older in 1965, only 5% had completed four years of college or more. By 2023, this share had risen to 33%.[2]

More older adults can meet their daily care needs. Older adults are functioning better on their own, and a shrinking share are living in nursing homes and assisted living settings than a decade ago. Home modifications and assistive devices, such as walkers, have helped older Americans maintain their independence.[3]

Gains in life expectancy recently stalled. U.S. life expectancy at birth declined by 2.4 years between 2019 and 2021.[4] The drop in life expectancy was driven largely by the COVID-19 pandemic, but deaths from

---

1 Analysis of data from the U.S. Census Bureau, Current Population Survey.

2 Analysis of data from the U.S. Census Bureau, Current Population Survey.

3 VA Freedman and JC Cornman, *National Health and Aging Trends Study: Trends Dashboards*, University of Michigan - Michigan Center on the Demography of Aging, 2023. https://micda.isr.umich.edu/research/nhats-trends-dashboards/.

4 *Life Expectancy Increases, However Suicides Up in 2022*, National Center for Health Statistics -NCHS Pressroom, November 29, 2023. https://www.cdc.gov/nchs/pressroom/releases/20231129.html?CDC_AAref_Val=https://www.cdc.gov/nchs/pressroom/nchs_press_releases/2023/20231129.htm.

drug overdoses, heart disease, chronic liver disease and cirrhosis, and suicide also played a role. Life expectancy rebounded slightly in 2022, to 77.5 years, but not enough to offset the decline during the pandemic.

Wide economic disparities are found across different population subgroups. Among adults ages 65 and older, 17% and 18% of those identifying as Latino and African American, respectively, lived in poverty in 2022, more than twice the rate of those who identified as non-Hispanic white (8%).[5]

More older adults are divorced compared with previous generations. The share of divorced women ages 65 and older increased from 3% in 1980 to 15% in 2023, and for men from 4% to 12% during the same period.[6]

More older women are living alone. Over one-fourth (27%) of women ages 65 to 74 lived alone in 2023. This share jumped to 39% among women ages 75 to 84, and to 50% among women ages 85 and older.[7]

Social Security and Medicare expenditures will increase from a combined 9.1% of gross domestic product in 2023 to 11.5% by 2035 because of the large share of older adults.[8]

Federal budget cuts and tax increases may be inevitable as more members of the large baby boom cohort reach retirement age and become eligible for entitlement programs. Policymakers can invest resources today to reduce poverty and improve the economic outlook for workers. These investments can increase young workers' future productive capacities and help offset the costs of an aging population.

---

5 *Historical Poverty Tables: People and Families - 1959 to 2024*, The United States Census Bureau, n.d.

https://www.census.gov/data/tables/time-series/demo/income-poverty/historical-poverty-people.html.

6 Trustees' report summary. Accessed January 20, 2026. https://www.ssa.gov/oact/TRSUM/.

7 Trustees' report summary. https://www.ssa.gov/oact/TRSUM/.

8 Trustees' report summary. https://www.ssa.gov/oact/TRSUM/.

INTRODUCTION

For many baby boomers, life brings a blend of exciting opportunities and unexpected challenges. I wrote this book to speak to those experiences, understanding that so many in this generation are facing situations they never quite anticipated. Just as we plan carefully for a career, sometimes we need to adjust and rethink how we manage our retirement. Navigating this stage of life calls for practical, thoughtful strategies and a bit of guidance along the way.

"Twenty Years from now, you will be more disappointed by things you didn't do than by the ones you did do."- Mark Twain

CHAPTER 1

Who is the Baby Boom Generation?

The U.S. population aged 66 and older, largely comprising the baby boom generation (born between 1946 and 1964), is defined by its significant size and increased longevity. In 2025, baby boomers are between 61 and 79 years old.

DEMOGRAPHICS

- **Population size and growth**: In 2022, 57.8 million Americans were aged 65 or older, accounting for 17.3% of the U.S. population. This group is projected to expand to 22% by 2040, driven by the aging baby boomers and increased life expectancy.
- **Gender distribution**: Women outnumber men in this age bracket. In 2022, the ratio for those 65 and older was 123 women to every 100 men. This gap widens with age, reaching 184 women for every 100 men among those 85 and older.
- **Growing diversity**: The older population is becoming more racially and ethnically diverse. The share of older adults identifying as non-Hispanic white is projected to decrease from 75% in 2022 to 60% by 2050.
- **Geographic distribution**: As of 2022, half of all people 65 and older lived in nine states: California, Florida, Texas, New York, Pennsylvania, Ohio, Illinois, North Carolina, and Michigan.

FINANCES

- **Income sources:** Social Security is a crucial income source for this age group, providing at least 50% of the income for over a third of older men and more than 40% of older women. Pensions are another common source of income.
- **Median income**: In 2022, the median income for Americans aged 65 and older was $29,740.
  However, a significant gender gap exists, with a median income of $37,430 for men compared to $24,630 for women.
- **Economic security and poverty**: While the overall poverty rate for those 65 and older has fallen significantly over the past 50 years, millions still face economic insecurity. This is reflected in the Supplemental Poverty Measure (SPM), which includes non-discretionary medical costs, providing a more comprehensive view than the standard poverty measure.[9]

LIFE & CONNECTIONS

- **Working Longer**: The retirement timeline is changing, with more older adults choosing to stay in the workforce. In 2023, approximately 11.2 million Americans aged 65+ were in the labor force.
- **Deeper Bonds:** Many older adults find that their relationships become more rewarding over time. They focus on the most meaningful connections and are more adept at managing social conflicts than their younger counterparts.
- **Living Choices**: In 2023, nearly 60% of older adults shared their home with a spouse or partner, while a significant portion (28%) lived alone, highlighting diverse living preferences.

9 https://www.census.gov/topics/income-poverty/supplemental-poverty-measure.html.

- **The Push for Independence**: With many desiring to "age in place," the market for supportive services like in-home care and medical alert systems is expanding rapidly.

HEALTH & LONGEVITY

- **Reaching a Plateau in Life Expectancy:** For those reaching age 65 in 2022, life expectancy was an additional 18.9 years, but recent trends show that this number has ceased to climb.[10]
- **Managing Multiple Conditions**: A high percentage of older adults, almost 80% of those 60 and older, live with two or more chronic illnesses. For many, heart disease poses the greatest risk.[11]
- **The Power of Prevention**: A focus on preventative care, including a healthy diet, exercise, and regular check-ups, is key to maintaining health and quality of life.
- **Sharp Minds, Positive Outlooks**: Social engagement, mentally challenging activities, and stress management are critical for preventing cognitive decline and preserving a positive mindset throughout the aging process.

The Administration for Community Living, which includes the Administration on Aging, is an operating division of the U.S. Department of Health and Human Services.

As members of the Silent Generation (1928–1945) age, we're approaching what is likely to be one of the largest transfers of wealth in history. For many Baby Boomers and Generation Xers, this may be the first time they have experienced a significant inheritance, and it brings both opportunity and responsibility.

10 https://www.census.gov/topics/income-poverty/supplemental-poverty-measure.html.

11 https://www.census.gov/topics/income-poverty/supplemental-poverty-measure.html.

Planning thoughtfully can make all the difference. Having an up-to-date estate plan and a clear succession strategy helps ensure that wealth passes smoothly, while minimizing unnecessary taxes or complications. I often encourage adult children to have open, compassionate conversations with their parents, working together to create a plan that honors their family's values and supports a seamless transition from one generation to the next. It's not just about finances; it's about preserving a legacy and peace of mind for everyone involved.

We will discuss estate planning in future chapters, so please keep reading.

The following graph displays the twentieth and twenty-first generations of population and their respective categories.

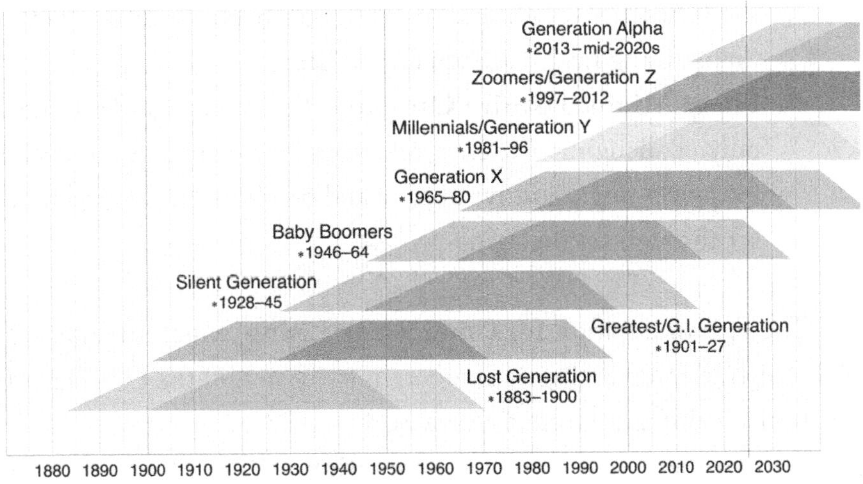

File: Generation timeline.svg - Wikimedia Commons

Over the years, I've had the privilege of working closely with countless individuals and families, helping them navigate the often-complicated world of finance. Through these experiences, I've learned what truly makes a difference in people's financial lives, and I want to share that with you.

This book comes from my heart and my years of experience in financial services. My goal is to offer practical, actionable guidance that can help you take control of your finances, make confident decisions, and feel more secure about your future. It's not just about numbers; it's about giving you the tools and understanding to improve your financial well-being and find peace of mind along the way.

Life can be likened to a flight, from the initial takeoff to the final landing. Each stage of the journey, take-off, flight time, and landing, requires different skills and preparations. Just as a flight might face turbulence or unexpected technical issues, we, too, encounter challenges and setbacks. We overcome these "ups and downs" or obstacles, whether through relying on the support of others or finding strength within ourselves.

At the heart of human experience is a quest for happiness, well-being, and financial stability. These aspirations are deeply tied to how we feel about ourselves, our circumstances, and our place in society.

This quest for security does not end in retirement; on the contrary, it continues. Empowerment comes in many different forms. Empowering yourself in your retirement years is an ongoing process of redefining your purpose, nurturing your physical and mental health, strengthening social connections, and securing your financial stability. This stage of life, which can bring uncertainty, is also an opportunity for personal growth, reinvention, and living on your own terms.

Retirement is a significant milestone; it marks the close of one chapter and the start of another, full of opportunities to explore passions, interests, and values that may have taken a back seat during your working years. With work no longer shaping your daily routine, finding new ways to feel purposeful and engaged can be incredibly rewarding.

Taking care of your physical health plays a big role in this next stage of life. Feeling strong and capable not only supports your independence but also boosts confidence and allows you to fully enjoy the activities you love. Your well-being, both physical and emotional, is deeply connected, and nurturing your body can make a real difference in how you experience retirement.

At the same time, having a sense of financial stability can provide peace of mind. With thoughtful planning, managing debt, building a solid retirement plan, and making the most of tax-advantaged accounts, individuals may be better positioned to understand their financial choices and consider approaches for managing long-term financial responsibilities. In many ways, retirement is about creating a balance that lets you feel secure, confident, and free to enjoy this new chapter to its fullest.

If you are a boomer, it is important to realize the changes that come when you enter retirement. The psychological effects can be more challenging than any other obstacle you may face.

Here's an example of one of the many interactions I have had within my career.

While I was at a conference, an elderly couple met with my team. Upon my return, I was briefed on the meeting. My staff explained that the couple had substantial wealth but was resistant to paying fees or commissions. They viewed a follow-up as a waste of time, but I insisted on another meeting. I explained that the couple's visit was an invitation, not a refusal, and requested their file to prepare.

When the couple arrived, I greeted them, and the wife immediately stated, "Your staff tried to sell us an investment, and we aren't interested in paying a fee." I nodded and replied, "I've asked you here to offer you a job." The wife looked stunned. I continued, "You've done a phenomenal job accumulating this portfolio. Your knowledge of growing assets is impressive, and that's precisely why you're here."

I addressed the wife's concerns about her husband's impending required minimum distributions; she feared that drawing income from their portfolio would deplete their principal. After her husband shared a reassuring smile, I explained my value proposition, offering my expertise to construct a portfolio that could provide a steady income stream for their golden years without eroding their capital. When I proposed a clear and fair fee structure, the couple accepted. Eight years later, they remain valued clients.

> *"As the baby boomers like me are retiring and getting ready to retire, they will spend whatever it takes—and they're the wealthiest generation in our country—to make themselves live an enjoyable life in their retirement years."*
>
> —David Rubenstein

CHAPTER 2

Understanding Your Finances

In my last book, *The Art of Creating Wealth: A Millennial, Gen Z, and Gen X Guide to Navigating Life's Struggles*, I emphasized the importance of concepts like the time value of money, budgeting, and asset allocation. Those fundamentals remain unchanged. However, if you are in or approaching retirement, the application of these principles, particularly the time value of money, shifts. That's because factors like your time horizon and the ability to continue saving through employment begin to change significantly.

A clear understanding of your financial situation in retirement is crucial to maintaining stability, meeting your goals, and making informed decisions for the years ahead. You've worked hard to get here; now, it's time to take control of your retirement finances and create the freedom you deserve.

Below, I've listed what I have discovered to be the most important financial issues facing baby boomers. We will also discuss these matters in future chapters.

1. **Retirement Income Planning**
    - Ensuring a steady and sustainable income stream (e.g., Social Security, pensions, annuities, withdrawals from savings).
    - Deciding when to claim Social Security for optimal benefits.

2. **Healthcare Costs & Medicare**
    - Planning for out-of-pocket expenses, supplemental insurance, and long-term care.
    - Understanding Medicare enrollment, coverage, and potential gaps.
3. **Longevity Risk**
    - Making savings last potentially 25–30+ years in retirement.
    - Considering inflation, market volatility, and healthcare expenses over time.
4. **Estate Planning**
    - Creating or updating wills, trusts, powers of attorney, and healthcare directives.
    - Minimizing taxes and ensuring smooth wealth transfer to heirs.
5. **Tax Efficiency**
    - Managing taxes on retirement account withdrawals (e.g., RMDs from IRAs/401(k)s).
    - Utilizing Roth conversions or charitable giving strategies to reduce tax impact.
6. **Investment Management**
    - Adjusting portfolio risk with age (shifting to a more conservative allocation while remaining growth-oriented).
    - Diversification to protect against market downturns.
7. **Debt Management**
    - Paying off or managing mortgages, credit cards, and other debts before or during retirement.
8. **Lifestyle & Spending Adjustments**
    - Budgeting realistically for your retirement lifestyle.
    - Evaluating whether downsizing or relocating makes financial sense.

9. **Legacy & Gifting Goals**
    - Planning charitable contributions or gifts to children/grandchildren.
    - Balancing personal financial needs with legacy desires.
- **Cognitive Decline & Financial Safeguards:** Putting protections in place in case of diminished financial decision-making ability (trusted advisors, financial POAs, family involvement)

As a financial professional, I often see that retirement planning for baby boomers is deeply personal, shaped not just by numbers, but priorities, values, and life circumstances. As retirement nears, financial concerns tend to become more focused and concrete, less about theory and more about real-life decisions that affect daily living and long-term security.

For most boomers, the top priority is ensuring a steady and reliable income. The worry of outliving one's savings is very real, and it makes sense. After decades of regular paychecks, the shift to living off savings and retirement accounts can feel daunting. This is why careful planning around Social Security, withdrawals from retirement accounts, and creating a strategy that balances spending with longevity is so important. The goal is simple: to make sure your resources can support you comfortably for the years ahead.

Closely following income planning is the concern over healthcare costs. As we age, medical needs tend to increase, and expenses can be significant. Understanding Medicare, when to enroll, what it covers, and how to supplement it becomes critical. Many retirees are surprised to discover how much may still come out of pocket, particularly for prescriptions or long-term care. That's why healthcare planning is not just a medical consideration; it's a core part of financial planning, essential to protecting both your health and your financial well-being.

By approaching these decisions thoughtfully and proactively, retirees can create a plan that offers peace of mind, confidence, and the ability to enjoy this next chapter fully.

Once these immediate concerns are addressed, many retirees begin thinking about risks specifically, how to protect themselves from market volatility, inflation, and the uncertainties of a long retirement. Investment strategies often become more conservative, but they still need to generate enough growth to keep pace with rising costs. The balance between protecting wealth and maintaining purchasing power becomes a central theme.

For those further into retirement, or who feel more financially secure, attention turns toward legacy planning. Estate planning, gifting to children or grandchildren, and charitable giving come into sharper focus. These concerns are often deeply personal and value-driven, reflecting a desire to make a meaningful impact or ensure family security

Interestingly, some of the most important financial matters, like tax strategy or long-term care planning, are often delayed or overlooked simply because they don't feel urgent. Unless someone is working with a financial advisor who brings these topics forward, they may not get the attention they deserve until a triggering event forces the issue.

Ultimately, how baby boomers prioritize their financial decisions is a dynamic process, evolving with age, health, market conditions, and personal goals. What matters most is building a financial plan that is flexible enough to shift as priorities change, because they inevitably will.

As baby boomers continue to retire in large numbers, understanding Social Security and how its benefits are taxed has become increasingly important. For many in this generation, Social Security represents a significant portion of their retirement income. Misunderstanding how benefits work, or how they are taxed, can lead to financial surprises, poor planning, and even unnecessary hardship.

First and foremost, knowing how Social Security works allows baby boomers to make informed decisions about when to claim benefits. Claiming early may reduce monthly payments for life, while delaying benefits increases them. Understanding these trade-offs helps retirees maximize their income based on their individual needs, health, and life expectancy.

Retirement is often viewed as the reward for a lifetime of hard work; it's a time to relax, travel, and enjoy the fruits of your labor. However, managing finances in retirement can be more complex than many people realize. One of the most critical yet overlooked aspects is tax planning. For this reason, working with a qualified tax planner in retirement is not just beneficial; it can be essential for maintaining long-term financial health.

Awareness of how Social Security benefits are taxed is important. Many people mistakenly believe that Social Security income is always tax-free. Depending on a retiree's total income, including pensions, wages, dividends, or withdrawals from retirement accounts, *up to 85% of Social Security benefits can be subject to federal income tax.* This taxation can significantly affect a retiree's take-home income and their overall financial strategy.

Additionally, planning around taxation can help baby boomers avoid higher Medicare premiums or being pushed into a higher tax bracket. By understanding how different types of income interact with Social Security, retirees can structure their withdrawals and investments more effectively to minimize tax burdens.

A major reason to consult a tax planner is that retirement does not mean an end to taxes. In fact, retirees often face a complicated tax landscape. Income may come from various sources, such as Social Security, pensions, retirement accounts (like IRAs or 401(k)s), investment portfolios, rental properties, or part-time work. Each of these income sources can be taxed differently, and their interaction can impact not only a retiree's tax bill but also things like Medicare premiums and eligibility for certain credits or benefits.

A qualified tax planner can help retirees navigate these complexities. They are trained to analyze an individual's entire financial picture and recommend strategies that can reduce unnecessary tax burdens. For example, a tax planner might suggest when and how much to withdraw from retirement accounts to stay in a lower tax bracket, or how to minimize the taxation of Social Security benefits. They may also recommend Roth conversions, charitable giving strategies, or tax-efficient investment withdrawals to create a more favorable tax outcome.

Beyond saving money, working with a tax planner may help you feel more confident. The tax code is constantly changing, and retirees may not have the time, expertise, or interest to keep up with new rules and regulations. A qualified professional can provide guidance tailored to a retiree's specific goals and adjust their strategy as laws or life circumstances change.

Retirement brings both freedom and financial responsibility. Partnering with a qualified tax planner may help retirees to make smarter decisions, reduce tax liability, and protect their hard-earned savings. Rather than guessing about the details of their financial circumstances or risking costly mistakes, retirees can potentially enjoy their golden years with greater confidence and financial security.

"Retirement at 65 is ridiculous. When I was 65, I still had pimples."

— George Burns

CHAPTER 3

Social Security / Medicare

The U.S. **Social Security** system is a federal program that provides financial benefits to retired workers, disabled individuals, and surviving family members of deceased workers. Funded through payroll taxes under the Federal Insurance Contributions Act (FICA), Social Security offers monthly payments based on a person's earnings history and the age at which they begin claiming benefits, starting as early as age 62.

Medicare is a separate federal health insurance program primarily for people aged 65 and older, though some younger individuals with disabilities may also qualify. It is divided into different parts:

- **Part A** covers hospital stays, nursing facility care, hospice care, and some home health care, and is usually premium-free.
- **Part B** covers doctor visits and outpatient care and supplies (doctor visits, preventative care, medical equipment, and some prescription drugs) and requires a monthly premium.
- **Part C** (Medicare Advantage) is an alternative that bundles Parts A and B and often includes additional benefits (hospital care, doctor visits, and medical tests). It may include dental, vision, hearing, and prescription drug coverage.
- **Part D** is optional, private insurance that provides prescription drug coverage.

Together, Social Security and Medicare form the foundation of retirement and health security for millions of Americans.

Deciding when to begin receiving Social Security benefits is one of the most important financial choices a retiree will make. While benefits can be claimed as early as age 62, delaying them can lead to significantly higher monthly payments. This decision is not one-size-fits-all. Several personal and financial factors must be weighed carefully to determine the best time to start collecting Social Security.

One of the primary considerations is life expectancy. Social Security is designed to pay out roughly the same total amount over a person's lifetime, regardless of when benefits are claimed. However, if someone expects to live well into their eighties or beyond, due to good health or family history, waiting to claim benefits can result in a higher lifetime payout. On the other hand, individuals with serious health concerns may benefit more from claiming early, even though monthly payments will be permanently reduced.

Financial need is another crucial factor. Some people may not have enough savings or other income sources to cover basic living expenses in their early sixties. In these cases, taking Social Security early can provide necessary financial support. However, those who can afford to wait, especially if they are still working or have other income, might benefit from delays.

The Full Retirement Age (FRA) is a key point in this decision. FRA varies based on birth year but is typically between 66 and 67 for today's retirees. Claiming benefits before your FRA results in a reduction of up to 30%, depending on how early you start. Conversely, for every year you delay past your FRA, up to age 70, your benefit increases by about 8% annually due to delayed retirement credits. Waiting until age 70 is the latest you can delay benefits and receive these increases.

Marital status also plays a role. For example, married couples may benefit from coordinating when each spouse claims benefits to maximize survivor benefits. Widows, widowers, and divorcees may also have unique options that affect timing decisions.

Additionally, employment status matters. If you claim Social Security before your FRA and continue working, your benefits may be temporarily reduced if you earn over a certain limit. This is known as the "earnings test," and it can impact those who want to retire gradually or take on part-time work.

The decision to take Social Security early or wait depends on a variety of personal factors, including life expectancy, financial needs, employment plans, and marital status. While it's possible to start as early as age 62, delaying up to age 70 can result in significantly larger monthly payments. To make the best choice, individuals should evaluate their long-term financial goals and, if possible, consult with a financial advisor or Social Security expert.[12]

Medicare is a vital part of retirement planning, providing essential health coverage for millions of Americans aged 65 and older. However, knowing when to enroll and whether enrollment is necessary if you're still working can be confusing. Making the wrong choice can result in late enrollment penalties or gaps in coverage. Therefore, it is important to understand the rules and exceptions surrounding Medicare enrollment.

Most people become eligible for Medicare at age 65. The initial enrollment period (IEP) begins three months before the month of your 65th birthday, includes your birthday month, and extends for three months after—a total of seven months. During this time, you can sign up for Medicare Part A (hospital insurance) and Part B (medical insurance) without penalty.

However, if you are still working at age 65 and have employer-sponsored health coverage, you may not be required to enroll in Medicare

12 *Retirement Benefits*, Social Security. Accessed November 21, 2025. http://www.ssa.gov/retirement.

right away. In this case, whether you must enroll depends on the size of your employer:

- If your employer has 20 or more employees, you can usually delay enrolling in Medicare Part B without penalty, since your employer's health plan is considered "creditable coverage."
- If your employer has fewer than 20 employees, you generally must enroll in Medicare Part A and B at 65, because Medicare becomes the primary payer, and your employer coverage becomes secondary.

Most people choose to enroll in Medicare Part A at 65 even if they are still working, since it is usually premium-free (assuming you or your spouse paid Medicare taxes for at least 10 years). However, if you're contributing to a Health Savings Account, enrolling in Part A can disqualify you from making further contributions.

If you delay Medicare because you're still working and covered by a qualifying group plan, you'll have a Special Enrollment Period (SEP) when that coverage ends. This SEP lasts for 8 months from your coverage end date, during which time you can enroll in Part B without a late penalty.

While Medicare enrollment typically begins at age 65, it's not always mandatory if you're still working and have qualifying health coverage. Knowing the rules around enrollment can help you avoid costly penalties and ensure a smooth transition into Medicare when the time is right. It's often wise to consult with a Medicare expert or HR representative to understand how your current coverage interacts with Medicare before making a final decision.

If you are employed after enrolling in Social Security or Medicare, you are still subject to FICA taxes, regardless of whether you're already receiving benefits.

What Is FICA?

FICA stands for the Federal Insurance Contributions Act, and it funds:

- Social Security (OASDI – Old-Age, Survivors, and Disability Insurance)

Medicare (HI – Hospital Insurance)

As long as you're working for an employer (not self-employed), both you and your employer must pay FICA taxes on your wages.

FICA Taxes in Detail:

Tax	Employee Rate	Employer Rate	Total
Social Security	6.2% (up to income cap: $168,600 in 2024)	6.2%	12.4%
Medicare	1.45%	1.45%	2.9%
Additional Medicare Tax	+0.9% (on income above $200,000 for individuals)	N/A	N/A

Key Points:

- Receiving Social Security or Medicare benefits does *not* exempt you from FICA taxes.
- Even if you're past Full Retirement Age and drawing Social Security, if you're earning a paycheck, you're still contributing.
- The same applies to Medicare: Enrolling in Medicare (even if it's only Part A) does not stop FICA taxes from being withheld from your paycheck.
- If you're self-employed, you pay both the employer and employee portion (15.3% total) as part of the self-employment tax.

Continuing to work and pay into Social Security may increase your future benefits if your new earnings replace lower-earning years in your benefit calculation.

While many view Social Security benefits as a retirement entitlement, the reality is that Social Security is a tax imposed on all income earners. Originally, Social Security was not designed to provide benefits to everyone, but rather to serve as a safety net for individuals, particularly those at risk of poverty in old age, with a disability, or through the loss of a family breadwinner.

Social Security is often viewed as a universal benefit, one that all workers contribute to throughout their careers and expect to receive in retirement. Despite having accumulated significant personal wealth, millionaires and wealthy individuals may feel entitled to Social Security benefits for several reasons.

1. Social Security contributions are mandatory for nearly all workers through payroll taxes. Since these taxes are deducted from their wages or salaries, wealthy individuals see their benefits as a direct return on what they have paid into the system over the years. Unlike voluntary retirement savings or investments, Social Security is a compulsory program, and many view it as an earned right rather than a welfare benefit.
2. Many wealthy individuals have worked for decades and contributed significant amounts to Social Security, which makes them feel they have a legitimate claim to the benefits. The program is based on a worker's earnings record, so higher earners pay more in payroll taxes and thus receive higher benefits, reinforcing their sense of entitlement.
3. Lastly, Social Security also serves purposes beyond retirement income; it provides disability benefits, survivor benefits for families, and a safety net that supports many Americans in times of need. Wealthy individuals may view these protections as part of

the social contract they have contributed to throughout their working lives.

It's important to understand how Social Security benefits are taxed. Up to 85% of Social Security income can be taxable if a retiree's combined income exceeds certain thresholds, $25,000 for individuals and $32,000 for married couples filing jointly. "Combined income" is calculated by adding adjusted gross income, non-taxable interest, and half of the Social Security benefits received. When a retiree's income exceeds these limits, Social Security benefits can be taxed at ordinary income tax rates, potentially increasing the overall tax burden.

Wealthy individuals often manage their taxable income carefully to avoid pushing their Social Security benefits into higher tax brackets. One common approach involves controlling the sources of retirement income to reduce taxable income. For example, instead of withdrawing funds from traditional IRAs or 401(k)s, which are taxed upon distribution, retirees may withdraw from Roth IRAs or Roth 401(k)s, where qualified withdrawals are tax-free. By prioritizing tax-free income sources, they can keep their adjusted gross income lower, thereby minimizing Social Security benefit taxation.

Another key strategy is managing required minimum distributions (RMDs) from traditional retirement accounts. Beginning at age 73, retirees must withdraw a minimum amount annually from traditional IRAs and 401(k)s, which increases taxable income and can cause more of their Social Security benefits to be taxed. Wealthy individuals may convert traditional IRA funds to Roth IRAs before reaching RMD age, as Roth IRAs do not require minimum distributions, and qualified withdrawals are tax-free. This reduces future taxable income and helps preserve the non-taxable status of their Social Security benefits.

Charitable giving also plays a significant role in tax planning for retirees. Through Qualified Charitable Distributions (QCDs), individuals over

70½ can donate directly from their IRAs to charity. These distributions count toward RMDs but are excluded from taxable income, effectively lowering adjusted gross income. This approach helps keep Social Security benefits below taxable thresholds while supporting philanthropic goals.

Lastly, wealthy retirees often strategically time the realization of capital gains and other income. By spreading out income and capital gains over multiple years, they avoid income spikes that could increase the taxability of Social Security benefits in any single year.

While Social Security benefits are subject to taxation based on overall income, wealthy individuals often employ a combination of tax-efficient strategies to reduce or avoid these taxes. By carefully managing withdrawals, utilizing Roth accounts, engaging in charitable giving, and timing income, they can minimize the impact of taxes on their retirement income and preserve more of their Social Security benefits. These approaches highlight the importance of comprehensive tax planning in achieving a secure and tax-efficient retirement.

It appears that the system disproportionately benefits the wealthiest members of society. Unfortunately, politicians in Washington, often influenced by donations from these affluent individuals, tend to protect their interests by resisting necessary reforms to the welfare program.

In addition, Congress should enact a law allowing Social Security recipients to decline Social Security benefits. The idea that anyone must take their Social Security benefit at 70 years old is absurd.

According to the 2025 Social Security Board of Trustees' annual report,[13] the surplus in the trust funds that disburse retirement, disability, and other Social Security benefits will be depleted by 2034.[14]

---

13 The 2025 Oasdi Trustees Report. Accessed November 22, 2025. https://www.ssa.gov/OACT/TR/2025/index.html.

14 Kenneth Terrell, *Social Security Report Projects Trust Fund Shortfall in 2034*. AARP, June 18, 2025. https://www.aarp.org/social-security/trust-fund-shortfall-projected-2034/.

That's one year earlier than the trustees projected in their 2024 report.[15]

A 2021 survey by Nationwide found that roughly four in five millennials and Gen Xers were concerned about Social Security running out of funding in their lifetimes. Many Boomers, many of whom were already receiving checks, said they were worried that they would stop getting monthly payments. Nearly half of Millennials indicated they believed they wouldn't get a penny in Social Security benefits.

Social Security will not be depleted in 2033; the OASI Trust Fund will. Should that happen, retirees would still receive approximately 76% of their benefits. That's because your monthly check is paid for by the payroll taxes of current workers as well as by the trust. In other words, if Americans are working and paying taxes, Social Security will continue to pay out benefits, even if the benefits are somewhat reduced from current levels.

I recall a client meeting with Joe, who was uncertain whether to begin collecting his Social Security benefits or delay them until reaching his full retirement age. At the time, he was 62, which meant he would receive a reduced benefit if he elected to start early.

I explained that this decision is not a matter of right or wrong, but rather a personal choice that should align with his individual financial needs and long-term goals. It is a decision that requires confidence and a "no-looking-back" mindset once made.

I also informed him that by age 70, he would be required to begin taking his benefits, as delaying beyond that point is not permitted. He felt a part-time job delivering auto parts and his Social Security benefit at 62 was the right choice for him. He felt that with the savings he had accumulated from his employment over the years and his spouse's

---

15 Andy Markowitz, *Social Security Trustees Project Fund Shortfall in 2035*. AARP, May 7, 2024. https://www.aarp.org/social-security/trust-fund-shortfall/.

full-time job with health insurance, and no significant debt, they could make it work.

A matter of personal preference.

Politicians will need to address the problem, either through benefit cuts or tax hikes. Evidence suggests Americans may prefer the latter.

Preserving the system while ensuring wealthy individuals can live comfortably requires a strong commitment and the willingness to face difficult challenges. One way to "think out of the box" could be not taxing retirees' similar retirement account distributions at the same level as Social Security benefits. For example, if a retiree with $3 million in a qualified account took a withdrawal identical to his or her Social Security benefit tax-free, any additional funds withdrawn would be taxable at the appropriate tax rate. This tax-free withdrawal would be instead of a Social Security benefit.

Finally, another option should be a discounted present value lump sum payout rather than a fully taxable annuity option. In other words, if a fully insured 66-year-old individual is expected to receive a $3,000 monthly benefit, the Social Security Administration should provide a lump sum option only if the individual has substantial other benefits or assistance available through an employer plan or other qualified plan.

No, Social Security isn't going bankrupt, but you can still do more to better fund your golden years. That way, you're prepared for a fulfilling retirement, no matter what Social Security is paying out.

"The harder you work, the harder it is to surrender."

—Vince Lombardi.

CHAPTER 4

Healthcare Considerations

As I stated previously, retirement marks a significant life transition, often filled with dreams of relaxation, travel, and personal fulfillment. However, one of the most critical, and sometimes overlooked, aspects of planning for retirement is healthcare. As individuals age, medical needs tend to increase, making healthcare a central component of financial and lifestyle planning. Without proper preparation, healthcare costs can quickly become a financial burden, affecting both quality of life and retirement security. Therefore, understanding and addressing healthcare considerations is essential for a smooth and secure retirement.

One of the first healthcare considerations in retirement is health insurance coverage. In the United States, most people become eligible for Medicare at age 65. Medicare provides a foundational level of health insurance, but it does not cover everything. For instance, it excludes most dental, vision, hearing, and long-term care services.

Retirees must decide whether to rely solely on Original Medicare or opt for additional coverage through Medicare Advantage plans or supplemental insurance (Medigap). These additional policies help cover deductibles, co-payments, and services not included in standard Medicare, providing more comprehensive protection against high medical costs.

Another major consideration is the cost of healthcare itself. Even with Medicare, out-of-pocket expenses can be substantial. A

65-year-old couple retiring today may need hundreds of thousands of dollars to cover healthcare expenses throughout retirement. These costs include premiums, deductibles, co-pays, prescriptions, and other non-covered services. Planning for these expenses is crucial. This might involve contributing to a Health Savings Account (during working years), purchasing long-term care insurance, or setting aside dedicated savings for healthcare needs.

Long-term care is another critical area that requires attention. Many retirees will need assistance with daily living activities at some point, whether in the form of in-home care, assisted living, or nursing home services. Medicare does not often cover these services, and the costs can be staggering. Early planning, including exploring long-term care insurance or hybrid life insurance policies with long-term care riders, can help protect assets and ensure quality care when it's needed most.

In addition to financial considerations, retirees must also think about access to healthcare providers. After retirement, especially if relocating to a new area, individuals should ensure they have access to doctors and hospitals that accept Medicare or their insurance plan. Proximity to quality healthcare facilities becomes more important with age, especially for managing chronic conditions or emergencies.

Lastly, personal health and wellness should not be overlooked. Maintaining a healthy lifestyle in retirement can reduce the risk of illness and decrease medical costs over time. Regular exercise, a balanced diet, preventive care, and managing stress all contribute to better health outcomes and greater independence during retirement years.

Medicare is a federal health insurance program in the United States primarily for people aged 65 and older, though it also covers some younger individuals with disabilities or certain medical conditions.

It has four main parts:

- Part A (Hospital Insurance): Covers inpatient hospital care, skilled nursing facility care, hospice, and some home healthcare.
- Part B (Medical Insurance): Covers doctor visits, outpatient care, preventive services, and some home healthcare. It requires a monthly premium.
- Part C (Medicare Advantage): Offered by private insurance companies, these plans bundle Parts A and B, and often include additional benefits like vision, dental, and prescription drug coverage.
- Part D (Prescription Drug Coverage): Helps cover the cost of prescription medications. It's offered through private insurers and requires a monthly premium.

While Medicare covers many healthcare services, it doesn't cover everything, such as most dental, vision, hearing care, or long-term care, so retirees often supplement it with additional insurance.

One common option for dental and vision care in retirement is purchasing standalone dental and vision insurance policies. Many private insurers offer plans specifically for retirees that cover routine and some major dental procedures, as well as eye exams, glasses, and contact lenses. These policies often require monthly premiums and may have deductibles and co-pays, but they can significantly reduce out-of-pocket costs. It's important for retirees to carefully compare plans based on coverage, network providers, and costs to find a policy that meets their needs and budget.

Another avenue for coverage is Medicare Advantage plans (Part C). Unlike Original Medicare, many Medicare Advantage plans include additional benefits such as dental, vision, and even hearing care. These plans are offered by private companies approved by Medicare and often bundle hospital, medical, and prescription drug coverage with supplemental benefits. Retirees who want more comprehensive coverage should research the Medicare Advantage options available in their area to see if these benefits are included.

Some retirees may also consider discount plans or membership programs for dental and vision care. These programs are not insurance but offer discounted rates at participating providers. They can be an affordable way to reduce costs for routine care and procedures but typically do not provide the same level of financial protection as insurance.

While many retirees rely on Medicare for their healthcare needs, it does not cover all medical expenses, particularly long-term care. This is where Medicaid becomes especially important. Medicaid is a state and federally funded program that provides health coverage for people with limited income and resources. In retirement, Medicaid can play a vital role for individuals who need additional healthcare services or support beyond what Medicare offers.

Unlike Medicare, which is primarily age-based and available to most individuals aged 65 and older, Medicaid eligibility is based on financial need. Retirees who have low income and limited assets may qualify for Medicaid, either on their own or in combination with Medicare. Those who qualify for both programs are known as "dual eligibles." For these individuals, Medicaid can help pay for costs that Medicare does not cover, such as premiums, deductibles, and long-term care services.

One of the most significant benefits of Medicaid for retirees is its coverage of long-term care, including nursing home stays and in-home care assistance. These services are typically not covered by Medicare, which can leave retirees financially vulnerable if they need extended care. Medicaid steps in to provide support for these essential services, which are often costly and long-term in nature. Without Medicaid, many older adults would be unable to afford the care they need as they age.

To qualify for Medicaid in retirement, individuals must meet certain income and asset requirements, which vary by state. Generally, a retiree must have a low income and limited savings or property. However, states often exclude certain assets, such as a primary home or a personal vehicle, when determining eligibility. In addition to financial qualifications, retirees seeking long-term care benefits may also need to demonstrate a medical need, such as requiring assistance with daily living activities like bathing, dressing, or eating.

Each state administers its own Medicaid program, so the rules and coverage can differ depending on where a person lives. Some states have expanded Medicaid under the Affordable Care Act, making it more accessible to a broader range of individuals. Others may have stricter guidelines. It's important for retirees to understand their state's specific requirements and to seek guidance if they believe they might qualify.

As people grow older, many find themselves needing long-term care, support with daily tasks such as bathing, dressing, eating, and mobility. These services can be provided in nursing homes, assisted living facilities, or through in-home care. However, the costs of long-term care are high and are often not covered by Medicare, leaving many retirees unsure of how to pay for the care they need. This is where Medicaid, a joint federal and state program, becomes essential. Medicaid offers long-term care benefits to individuals who meet specific financial and medical eligibility requirements. Understanding these requirements is key to accessing the necessary support during retirement.

To qualify for Medicaid-funded long-term care, individuals must first meet strict financial criteria. These include limits on both income and assets. While the exact figures vary by state, in most cases, a single applicant must have extremely limited income, often less than $2,800 per month, and no more than $2,000 in countable assets. Countable assets include items such as cash savings, investments, and additional properties. However, Medicaid does not count certain essential assets when determining eligibility. For example, a person's primary home is usually excluded (especially if a spouse or dependent lives there), as is one vehicle, their personal belongings, and a small amount of life insurance. If an applicant's assets exceed the allowed amount, they may be required to spend down their resources before qualifying.

In addition to meeting financial requirements, applicants must also demonstrate a medical need for long-term care. This typically means they need help with several activities of daily living (ADLs), such as using the toilet, moving from a bed to a chair, feeding themselves, or managing medications. Each state conducts its own medical assessment to determine if a person meets the level of care required to qualify. Usually, the need must be comparable to the type of care provided in a nursing home.

Another important factor in Medicaid eligibility is the look-back period. To prevent individuals from transferring assets to family or friends to meet Medicaid's financial limits, the program reviews an applicant's financial transactions for the five years prior to the application. If any assets were given away or sold below market value during this time, Medicaid may impose a penalty period for long-term care and delay coverage.

For married couples, special rules are in place to prevent financial hardship for the spouse who is not applying for care, often referred to as the community spouse. Medicaid allows this spouse to keep a certain portion of the couple's joint income and assets, so they can continue living independently. These spousal protection rules vary by state but are an important safeguard for families.

As a licensed health insurance professional in New Jersey, I do not support transferring assets between generations solely to qualify for Medicaid benefits.

Explanation:

This statement reflects a careful and professional perspective on asset transfers in relation to Medicaid eligibility. Medicaid has strict financial limits, and some individuals may consider transferring money or property to family members to qualify. While this approach might seem helpful, it can be viewed as attempting to circumvent the rules and could potentially lead to penalties under Medicaid's five-year look-back period. It's important to approach these decisions thoughtfully and work with a knowledgeable professional to ensure compliance and protect long-term financial security.

By sharing this perspective, I aim to highlight the value of thoughtful, responsible financial planning and to caution against strategies that could raise legal or ethical concerns. My goal is to guide clients toward long-term solutions that are both compliant with the law and aligned with sound ethical standards, ensuring their financial decisions are secure, sustainable, and in their best interest.

As people plan for retirement, one of the most pressing concerns is how to afford long-term care if it becomes necessary. Traditional long-term care insurance was once the go-to solution, but it comes with several drawbacks, including rising premiums and the risk of never using the benefits. To address these concerns, many individuals are turning to hybrid long-term care insurance policies, which combine life insurance with long-term care coverage.

A hybrid long-term care policy offers a unique structure. Instead of being a "use-it-or-lose-it" plan like traditional long-term care insurance, it provides multiple layers of financial protection. The policyholder pays a premium, either as a lump sum or over a set number of years, and in return, the policy guarantees benefits in three potential forms. First, if the individual needs long-term care, the policy provides tax-free funds to cover qualified care expenses, such as home care, assisted living, or nursing home services. Second, if the person never requires long-term care, the policy pays out a death benefit to their chosen beneficiaries. Third, many hybrid policies also offer a return-of-premium feature, allowing the policyholder to cancel the policy and receive a portion or all of their money back, depending on the terms.

Hybrid universal life policies that allow lump sum premiums are a standout example of hybrid policies that offer these benefits. They are designed to provide financial certainty and flexibility, with fixed premiums and guaranteed coverage. This means that policyholders do not have to worry about premium increases in the future, something that has become a common problem with traditional long-term care insurance. Additionally, policies are permanently life-insured, with a long-term care rider added on. The long-term care benefit typically exceeds the original premium paid, giving the policyholder access to more care dollars than they initially invested.

One of the strongest appeals of hybrid policies is their built-in value. If long-term care is needed, the policy helps protect a person's savings from being depleted by high care costs. If care is not needed, the death benefit ensures that the money goes to the policyholder's heirs. And if the policyholder changes their mind or their financial situation changes, they may have the option to surrender the policy for a refund (subject to terms and conditions). This triple benefit structure, long-term care coverage, life insurance payout, and return-of-premium flexibility, makes hybrid policies an attractive option for many retirees.

However, there are some important considerations. Hybrid policies often require higher upfront costs compared to traditional long-term care insurance. Because of this, they may not be suitable for individuals who need to keep their assets liquid or who cannot afford to make a large one-time payment. Also, if the long-term care benefit is used extensively, the death benefit may be reduced or eliminated, since the policy is designed to draw down the life insurance value to pay for care.

Despite these considerations, hybrid long-term care insurance policies have become a popular tool in retirement planning. They provide a comprehensive, flexible, and secure solution for managing the risk of long-term care while still offering financial protection for one's family. For individuals who want to avoid the uncertainty of traditional long-term care insurance and value the ability to pass on wealth or recover their investment, hybrid policies offer a smart, balanced alternative.

Retirement marks a significant transition in life, often providing individuals with the freedom to pursue passions and interests that may have been sidelined during their working years. A healthy and exercise-filled lifestyle during retirement not only enhances physical well-being but also contributes to mental and emotional health.

As individuals age, maintaining physical activity becomes increasingly vital. Regular exercise helps combat the natural decline in muscle mass, bone density, and cardiovascular health that can accompany aging. Engaging in physical activities can reduce the risk of chronic illnesses such as heart disease, diabetes, and osteoporosis. Moreover, staying active promotes better mobility and flexibility, which are crucial for maintaining independence and a quality of life.

A healthy lifestyle in retirement can also significantly improve mental health. Physical activity is known to release endorphins, the body's natural mood lifters, which can alleviate symptoms of anxiety and depression. Engaging in social activities, such as group exercise classes or recreational sports, fosters connections and combats feelings of loneliness, which can often accompany retirement. Thus, an active lifestyle not only improves physical health but also nurtures emotional well-being.

The benefits of regular exercise extend beyond physical and mental health. Increased physical activity can lead to better sleep quality, enhanced cognitive function, and a stronger immune system. Many retirees report feeling more energized and motivated when they prioritize exercise in their daily routines. This renewed vitality can lead to a more fulfilling retirement, allowing you to engage in hobbies, travel, or volunteer work that you may have put on hold.

Furthermore, exercise can be a catalyst for personal growth and exploration. Trying new activities, such as yoga, dancing, or hiking, can introduce retirees to new skills and interests, encouraging a sense of achievement and joy. The social aspect of group activities can also lead to new friendships and a sense of community, enriching the retirement experience.

Regular exercise is a powerful tool in reducing the risk of chronic illnesses. It promotes overall health and well-being, emphasizing the importance of incorporating physical activity into daily routines. If you're considering starting a new exercise program, it's always a good idea to consult with a healthcare professional, especially if you have existing health conditions.

Some conditions where exercise provides a protective role are as follows:

- Cardiovascular disease
  Regular physical activity helps improve heart health, lowers blood pressure, and may improve cholesterol levels.
- Type 2 diabetes
  Exercise helps regulate blood sugar levels, improves insulin sensitivity, and aids in weight management.
- Obesity
  Physical activity burns calories, promotes fat loss, and helps maintain a healthy weight.
- Osteoporosis
  Weight-bearing and resistance exercise strengthen bones and improve bone density.
- Depression and anxiety
  Regular physical activity can boost mood, reduce anxiety levels, and improve overall mental health.

Regular exercise is a powerful tool in reducing the risk of these chronic illnesses, promoting overall health and well-being, and emphasizing the importance of incorporating physical activity into daily routines. It also allows the body to rejuvenate, so injuries are less prone to occur.

Nutrition becomes crucial in maintaining health, managing weight, and preventing chronic diseases, making it essential for retirees to adopt dietary strategies that support their long-term well-being. One increasingly popular approach is intermittent fasting (IF), which has shown promise in enhancing health outcomes.

As individuals transition into retirement, their nutritional needs evolve. Aging often brings changes in metabolism, muscle mass, and overall health, necessitating a focus on nutrient-dense foods. A well-balanced diet rich in essential nutrients can help retirees maintain physical health, manage weight, and prevent chronic diseases.

When I worked with a qualified nutritionist during my own personal journey, I quickly realized how much our metabolism naturally slows as we age, making it easier to gain weight without noticing. Together, we focused on building a balanced approach to eating, choosing whole foods like fresh fruits, vegetables, whole grains, lean proteins, and healthy fats. Not only did this help me maintain a healthy weight, but it also gave me the nutrients my body needed to feel strong and energized.

I also learned how much of a difference small changes can make over time. Incorporating heart-healthy fats from fish, nuts, and olive oil while cutting back on processed foods and added sugars felt manageable, and it gave me confidence that I was supporting my long-term health. Working with a professional helped me see that eating well isn't just about weight, it's about reducing the risk of chronic conditions like heart disease, diabetes, and certain cancers, and creating a foundation for lasting vitality and wellness in retirement.

INTERMITTENT FASTING (IF)

Intermittent fasting is an eating pattern that alternates between periods of eating and fasting. Unlike traditional diets, IF does not prescribe specific foods; rather, it focuses on when to eat. Common methods of intermittent fasting include:

16/8 Method:

- This popular approach involves fasting for 16 hours and eating during an 8-hour window. For instance, an individual may choose to eat between noon and 8 p.m., allowing for a significant fasting period overnight and into the morning.

5:2 Diet:

- In this method, individuals eat normally for five days a week while restricting calorie intake to about 500-600 calories on two non-consecutive days. This approach allows for flexibility while promoting weight management and improved metabolic health.

My own personal journey on intermittent fasting is one I learned working with my nutritionist. I am on the 16/8 program. Your gut contains trillions of bacteria, forming a gut microbiome, that aids in digestion, nutrient production, immune system function, and metabolism regulation. As we age, our system weakens. It is essential to treat a weakened environment with care. A regular daily supplement of pre- and probiotics can assist with this.

The aid of supplements and intermittent fasting (IF) promotes a healthier gut microbiome by allowing microbes a period of rest, potentially increasing microbial diversity and fostering beneficial bacteria. This process may lead to beneficial shifts in gut bacteria, improved metabolic health, and enhanced gut barrier function.

Keep in mind that maintaining a healthy lifestyle is essential during one's life journey. In life as well as retirement, it is even more important; exercise and proper diet can contribute to a positive outcome.

"The economist John Maynard Keynes said that in the long run, we are all dead. If he were around today, he might say that, in the long run, we are all on Social Security and Medicare."

—Ben Bernanke

CHAPTER 5

Work After Retirement

When I think about retirement, I often hear people describe it as the long-awaited period to finally relax, travel, and enjoy the rewards of decades of hard work. And certainly, that's one part of it. But through my own experience and conversations with others, I've come to see that retirement doesn't always mean completely stepping away from work. For many, continuing to work in some capacity, whether part-time, freelance, or exploring a completely new venture, can bring unexpected and deeply rewarding benefits.

Personally, I've found that staying engaged professionally keeps life dynamic and purposeful. Work provides structure, a sense of accomplishment, and opportunities to challenge yourself in ways that relaxation alone sometimes can't. Beyond the practical financial benefits, continuing to work can be a source of personal fulfillment. It allows you to keep contributing your skills, experience, and knowledge, whether to a company, clients, or even your own creative projects. That feeling of making a difference, of leaving a mark, is incredibly energizing and rewarding.

There's also a social element that shouldn't be underestimated. Retirement can be isolating if your daily interactions are mostly gone, but staying professionally active, meeting colleagues, clients, or collaborators, helps maintain connections and build new ones. These interactions can bring both enjoyment and a sense of community, which is so important for overall well-being.

There are so many ways to remain active professionally in retirement. Some choose part-time roles in their original field, others explore freelance opportunities or consulting work, and some dive into entirely new passions or business ventures they've always wanted to pursue. Each option offers flexibility, a chance to learn, and the satisfaction of staying engaged in meaningful work.

For me, understanding the value of staying active after retirement has been transformative. It's not about prolonging work for the sake of money; it's about purpose, engagement, and the chance to continue growing. Retirement can be both a time of rest and a time of reinvention and finding the right balance between leisure and meaningful work can make this stage of life truly fulfilling.

REASONS FOR WORK AFTER RETIREMENT

1. Financial Security:

Many retirees seek to supplement their retirement income through part-time or freelance work. This can help cover living expenses, healthcare costs, and unexpected expenses that may arise as they age. Working can alleviate financial stress and provide a greater sense of security.[16]

Many retirees who golf might find employment as a "starter" at a local golf course, allowing them to feel comfortable in an environment where they flourish, and they can even play the course free of charge as a perk.

2. Continued Purpose and Identity:

For many, work is a significant part of their identity. Transitioning to retirement can lead to a loss of purpose, and continuing to work can

16 *The Importance of Financial Security in Retirement*, Journal of Financial Planning, 2020.

help maintain a sense of identity and fulfillment. Engaging in meaningful work can provide a sense of accomplishment and keep individuals mentally active.[17]

Many former contractors may search for employment at large box hardware stores or distributors, for instance, allowing them to remain active in the field in which they worked. A retired electrical contractor could get hired to aid customers in the electrical department.

3. Social Interaction:

Work environments offer valuable opportunities for social engagement. Continuing to work allows retirees to connect with colleagues and clients, reducing feelings of loneliness and isolation that can accompany retirement. Building and maintaining social relationships is crucial for emotional well-being.[18]

4. Staying Mentally and Physically Active:

Working can help retirees stay mentally sharp and physically active. Engaging in professional tasks requires problem-solving, critical thinking, and creativity, all of which can contribute to cognitive health. Additionally, many jobs involve physical activity, which is beneficial for maintaining overall health.[19]

Retired police officers may seek employment within school districts as resource officers. These positions require professional endorsement. Similarly, teachers may continue to tutor after retirement.

---

17 *Retirement and Identity: The Impact of Work on Self-Concept*, Gerontologist, 2018.

18 *Social Engagement and Its Impact on Well-Being in Older Adults*, Aging & Mental Health, 2016.

19 *The Role of Work in Promoting Cognitive Health in Older Adults*, Neuropsychology Review, 2019.

TYPES OF WORK AVAILABLE

1. Part-Time Employment:

Retirees can opt for part-time positions in their previous fields or in entirely new industries. Common part-time roles include consulting, teaching, retail, or administrative positions. These jobs provide flexibility while allowing retirees to leverage their skills and experience.[20]

2. Freelancing and Consulting:

Retirees can offer their expertise on a freelance basis, providing consulting services in their areas of knowledge. This allows for greater control over work hours and projects, making it an attractive option for those looking to maintain a work-life balance.[21]

3. Volunteering:

While not paid, volunteering can be a fulfilling way to stay engaged and make a difference in the community. Retirees can find great satisfaction in giving back, and through volunteer opportunities that can often provide social interaction and a sense of purpose.[22]

4. Entrepreneurship:

Some retirees pursue entrepreneurship by starting their own businesses. This option allows you to turn hobbies or passions into

---

20 *Part-Time Work in Retirement: Trends and Implications*, Work, Aging and Retirement, 2021.

21 *Freelancing After Retirement: Opportunities and Challenges*, Journal of Aging & Social Policy, 2019.

22 *The Benefits of Volunteering for Older Adults*, American Journal of Public Health, 2017.

income-generating ventures, offering both flexibility and the potential for personal fulfillment.[23]

ADVANTAGES OF WORKING AFTER RETIREMENT

1. Enhanced Quality of Life:

Engaging in work can significantly improve the quality of life in retirement. It provides structure, routine, and a sense of purpose that can enhance overall happiness and satisfaction.[24]

2. Social Connections:

Working allows retirees to maintain and build social connections, which are vital for emotional health. Social interactions at work can combat feelings of loneliness and increase overall life satisfaction.[25]

3. Continued Learning:

Working in retirement can also provide opportunities for lifelong learning and skill development. Whether through formal training or on-the-job experiences, retirees can continue to grow and adapt in a changing work environment.[26]

Working after retirement can offer numerous benefits, including financial security, continued purpose, social engagement, and cognitive and physical activity. Whether through part-time employment,

23 *Entrepreneurship in Later Life: A Growing Trend*, International Journal of Entrepreneurial Behavior & Research, 2020.

24 *Quality of Life in Retirement: Work, Leisure, and Health*, Journal of Happiness Studies, 2018.

25 *Social Connections and Mental Health in Retirement*, Psychology and Aging, 2020.

26 *Lifelong Learning and Its Impact on Older Adults*, Educational Gerontology, 2020.

freelancing, volunteering, or entrepreneurship, retirees have various avenues to explore that align with their interests and skills.

Embracing the opportunity to work in retirement can lead to a more fulfilling and enriching life, allowing you to thrive in this new chapter of your life. As society continues to evolve, the traditional view of retirement as a period of complete leisure is being redefined, paving the way for more active and engaged lifestyles.

As a financial consultant, I often see a growing number of professionals choosing to delay retirement and remain active in the workforce well into their seventies. This choice is motivated by a combination of financial considerations, a desire to stay engaged, and the pursuit of personal fulfillment.

From a financial perspective, continuing to work can be highly beneficial. Rising living costs, healthcare expenses, and the need for a stable, long-term income make it clear that delaying retirement can help ensure financial security. By working longer, individuals have the opportunity to continue contributing to retirement savings, maximize Social Security benefits, and strengthen their overall financial position, providing greater peace of mind for the years ahead.

Work often forms a central part of a person's identity. The roles professionals have held throughout their careers contribute to their self-worth and purpose. Transitioning to retirement can lead to feelings of loss and disorientation. Continuing to work allows people to maintain their professional identity and remain engaged in the activities that have defined their lives for decades, resulting in a sense of accomplishment and satisfaction.

The workplace serves as a vital social environment where we all connect or used to connect with colleagues and clients. Many retirees report feelings of loneliness and isolation after leaving the workforce. If you choose to continue working, you can maintain these important social connections and prevent the social withdrawal that can accompany retirement. Building and sustaining relationships in the workplace can enhance emotional well-being and provide a support system.

Continuing to work can keep your mind active and engaged, offering the joy of learning new skills and staying connected to your field. Mentoring younger colleagues can also bring a sense of purpose and fulfillment. Financially, working longer, even until 70, can boost retirement savings, maximize Social Security, and provide greater security for a comfortable lifestyle.

Not surprisingly, engaging in meaningful work can contribute to better overall health, too. The structure and routine that comes with work can help maintain a healthy lifestyle, promoting both mental and physical well-being.

Continuing to work in retirement helps maintain social connections and a sense of community, which are vital for emotional well-being and overall life satisfaction. It also allows experienced professionals to contribute their knowledge, mentor younger generations, and support both the workforce and the broader community, creating meaningful impact beyond personal fulfillment.

Working longer fosters social engagement and a sense of community. Remaining active in the workforce allows you to build relationships and maintain social networks, which are crucial for emotional health, can help you maintain a connection to your community, and enhance your overall life satisfaction and happiness.

Professionals who continue working contribute to the economy and society. Their experience and expertise can be invaluable in mentoring younger generations, driving innovation, and providing stability in the workforce. This contribution can have a positive impact on both the workplace and the community at large.

IMPLICATIONS FOR SOCIETY

From my perspective, the growing trend of professionals working into their seventies has interesting implications, not just for individuals, but for society. As more people stay in the workforce longer, businesses may need to adapt to support older employees, which can bring the added benefits of age diversity and inclusivity.

Organizations gain tremendously from the experience, knowledge, and perspective that seasoned professionals bring, often enhancing productivity and innovation. At the same time, as retirement ages shift, it may prompt adjustments to pension plans and Social Security policies, reflecting the evolving way people approach work and retirement today. Overall, this trend highlights the value of continued engagement, both personally and professionally, well into later years.

As the landscape of retirement continues to evolve, it is essential to recognize and support the valuable contributions of older professionals in the workforce. By embracing this trend, society can benefit from the experience and wisdom of an aging population, creating a more inclusive and productive environment for all.

At 67 years of age, I continue to find great fulfillment in the work I do. I have made it a priority to empower my staff to succeed by creating opportunities for them to grow and build meaningful careers. In doing so, I have intentionally reduced my share of the company's revenues to invest in its development and support the continued growth and longevity of the business.

"I can't wait to retire so I can get up at six o'clock in the morning and go drive around really slow and make everybody late for work."

— Unknown

CHAPTER 6

Business as a Source of Retirement Income

Business owners face yet another significant challenge: what to do with their business when they retire or in the unfortunate event of their passing. Should the business be sold or closed, or is there a succession plan in place to ensure a smooth transition?

Retirement is often viewed as the end of a professional journey, but for many entrepreneurs and business professionals, it is an opportunity to transition from active management to sustained wealth generation. One of the most strategic approaches to preparing for retirement is to build a lasting business arrangement based on existing business concepts. This involves transforming current operations, relationships, and intellectual capital into sustainable systems that continue to generate income long after one's active involvement has ceased. By drawing from proven business models, succession planning, and passive income strategies, entrepreneurs can create a retirement framework that preserves value, ensures legacy, and maintains financial independence.

As business owners approach retirement, they face a critical decision regarding the future of their enterprise(s).

This decision is not merely about stepping away from daily operations; it often involves determining the fate of a significant portion of their life's work. Owners typically consider several options, each with its advantages and challenges. Read on to explore the most common choices available to business owners when they retire, including selling the business, passing it to family members, closing the business, creating a succession plan, merging with another business, retaining a management role, franchising, and liquidating assets.

1. Selling the Business

One of the most straightforward options for business owners is to sell their business. This can be accomplished in several ways:

Sell to a Third Party: Owners may choose to sell their business to an external buyer, which could be an individual, a private equity firm, or another company. This option often provides immediate financial returns, allowing the owner to enjoy a comfortable retirement. The process involves valuing the business, marketing it to potential buyers, and negotiating a sale agreement. While selling to a third party can provide significant financial benefits, if you are in this boat, you must be prepared for the emotional challenges of letting go of a business you have built.

Sell to Employees: Another option is to sell the business to employees, often through an employee stock ownership plan (ESOP). This approach not only ensures that the business remains in capable hands but also rewards employees for their commitment and hard work. Selling to employees can create a sense of loyalty and continuity within the company, which can result in a more stable transition.

2. Selling Business to Family Members

Many business owners prefer to keep their enterprises within the family. Transferring ownership to family members can be a way to maintain the family legacy while ensuring that the business continues to thrive. However, this option requires careful planning to address potential conflicts and ensure that the successor is prepared to take on the responsibilities of ownership.

Family dynamics can complicate transitions, and owners need to communicate openly and set clear expectations. Many business owners may have one or two children who are not involved in the day-to-day business, but perhaps the business is the largest part of the estate. The business transition may require planning that addresses equalizing the estate so that all beneficiaries are treated fairly. This can be achieved with life insurance.

A business owner can purchase a life insurance policy through an ILIT (irrevocable life insurance trust) so that the business owner can act as the grantor of the trust, fund the premiums for the life insurance policy from proceeds of the business. The ILIT would own the policy and be the beneficiary of the policy. The death benefit would be a value equal to the business; upon the owner's passing, the policy would be directed to pay the proceeds to the children not involved in the business. This is a simplistic explanation of the structure, but it will require legal opinions and valuations.

3. Closing Business

In some cases, owners may decide to close their business, particularly if they believe it cannot be sold profitably or if there are no suitable successors. Closing a business involves winding down operations, fulfilling legal and financial obligations, and managing the emotional aspects of letting go. While this option may provide closure, it may also result in financial losses and unrealized potential.

4. Creating a Succession Plan

Creating a succession plan is a critical step for business owners to ensure a smooth transition when they retire or step down. Business owners can create a comprehensive succession plan that ensures a smooth transition and the continued success of the business. Proper planning not only protects the business but also promotes stability and confidence among employees and stakeholders during the transition.

I've taken steps to ensure the future of my business by creating a succession plan with one of my most trusted employees, whom I've made a partner. It's been incredibly rewarding to work closely with someone half my age, training them in every aspect of the business and seeing them become fully engaged and ready to carry the company forward. This process has given me confidence that the business, and the values I've built it on, will continue to thrive long into the future.

5. Merging with Another Business

Merging with another business can provide an exit strategy while allowing the original owner to remain involved in a reduced capacity. This option can enhance the new entity's resources and market presence, potentially leading to greater success than either company could achieve alone. Mergers can create synergies that benefit all parties involved, but they require careful negotiation and alignment of goals.

6. Maintaining a Management Role

Some owners choose to step back from daily operations but remain involved in a management or advisory role. This allows them to retain some connection to the business while enjoying retirement. Remaining in a part-time capacity can provide a sense of purpose and continuity for both the owner and the employees. This option can also facilitate a smoother transition, as the owner can offer guidance and support to the new leadership.

7. Franchising

For business owners with a successful model, franchising can be an attractive option. This approach allows them to expand their brand and generate income without actively managing every location. Franchising can provide a steady revenue stream and increased market presence while allowing the original owner to take a step back from daily operations. However, this option requires significant planning and investment in training and support for franchisees.

8. Liquidating Assets

In cases where selling the business is not feasible, owners may consider liquidating assets. This process involves selling off equipment, inventory, and other business assets to generate cash. While it may not yield as much as a full sale, it can provide some return on investment and allow owners to settle debts and obligations. Liquidation can be a necessary step when other options are not viable.

Business partnerships require careful planning, especially when one partner retires. In such cases, it is essential to address the influence and percentage of ownership that the retiring partner held, ensuring that appropriate steps are taken to manage the transition effectively.

In the realm of business partnerships, the establishment of a buy-sell agreement is a crucial step in ensuring a smooth transition of ownership among partners. This legally binding document outlines the specific terms under which a partner can sell their ownership stake, providing clarity and structure to what can often be a complex process. By clearly defining the conditions for selling, a buy-sell agreement helps prevent misunderstandings and disputes among partners, ultimately safeguarding the interests of all parties involved.

One of the fundamental aspects of a buy-sell agreement is the specification of how the business will be valued. This valuation process is essential, as it establishes a fair market price for the ownership stake being sold. Without a clear valuation method, partners may find themselves at odds over the worth of the business, leading to conflicts and potential financial losses. The agreement should delineate the approach to valuation, whether through a professional appraisal, a predetermined formula, or another method, so that all partners have a shared understanding of the business' worth.

Additionally, the buy-sell agreement should outline the process of selling an ownership stake. This includes the steps a partner must take to initiate a sale, the notification requirements to other partners, and any necessary approvals needed before proceeding with the transaction. By providing a structured process, the agreement minimizes the risk of hasty decisions that could negatively impact the business and its operations.

Moreover, it is essential for the agreement to include any restrictions on selling to outside parties. Such restrictions can prevent unwanted external influences and maintain the integrity of the partnership. For instance, partners may wish to establish a right of first refusal, allowing existing partners the opportunity to purchase the stake before it is offered to an outsider. This provision helps ensure that the business remains within the existing partnership or within trusted circles, preserving the company's culture and values.

Another critical element to consider in a buy-sell agreement is the incorporation of trigger events. These provisions address various scenarios that may necessitate a change in ownership, such as retirement, death, or the disability of a partner. By clearly defining the process that should be followed in these situations, the agreement provides clarity and structure, making all partners aware of their rights and obligations during potentially challenging times.

For example, in the event of a partner's retirement, the buy-sell agreement can outline the steps for valuing and selling their ownership stake, which can minimize disruptions to the business. Similarly, in the unfortunate event of a partner's death, the agreement can specify how the surviving partners should proceed with the transfer of ownership, protecting the interests of the deceased partner's heirs while honoring the existing partnership's dynamics.

One of the most important, but often overlooked, planning tools in our business is life insurance designed to protect a partnership. Many business owners focus on operations, growth, and day-to-day management, and the idea of planning for the unexpected can feel uncomfortable or abstract. Yet the sudden loss of a partner can create serious financial and operational challenges for the business and having a plan in place can make all the difference.

When we introduce the concept of partnership life insurance, it usually resonates immediately. It's not about anticipating the worst; it's about ensuring stability, continuity, and security for both the business and the remaining partners. With the right policy in place, the surviving partners are equipped to manage financial obligations, buy out a deceased partner's share if needed, and maintain the integrity of the business without disruption.

In my experience, once business owners understand how this works, they are eager to act. Implementing a plan not only protects the business but also provides peace of mind, knowing that the company, the relationships, and the legacy built within it are safeguarded no matter what the future holds.

Drafting a comprehensive buy-sell agreement is an essential aspect of managing a business partnership. By establishing clear terms for ownership transfers, outlining valuation processes, and including provisions for trigger events, partners can create a framework that facilitates easier transitions and protects the interests of all parties involved. This proactive approach not only minimizes potential conflicts but also encourages long-term stability and success of the business.

Retirement from actively participating in business need does not mean retirement from income, influence, or innovation. By leveraging existing business concepts such as franchising, licensing, intellectual property, succession planning, and strategic partnerships, entrepreneurs can create enduring business arrangements that support a comfortable and purpose-driven retirement.

Your goal is to transition from working in business to owning systems that work for the business. With foresight and strategic execution, the legacy of a lifetime's work can continue to thrive and provide lasting value well beyond the final working day.

"Everyone wants to live on top of the mountain, but all happiness and growth occur while you're climbing it."

—Andy Rooney

CHAPTER 7

Suitable Housing Options

As you transition into retirement, your housing needs can often change in response to lifestyle preferences, health considerations, and financial circumstances. Choosing the right housing arrangement is a critical decision that affects not only comfort and safety but also long-term well-being and independence. Fortunately, today you have a wide range of housing options available to suit diverse needs, from home ownership and rental units to independent living and assisted care environments.

One common option is aging in place, where retirees remain in their homes or downsize to a more manageable property. This choice is ideal for those who value independence and wish to stay connected to their community and familiar surroundings. Modifications such as installing handrails, ramps, or walk-in tubs can make your home safer and more accessible as you age. In-home care services can also be arranged as needed, allowing you to maintain autonomy while receiving support.

Another popular option is retirement communities or active adult communities. These are typically designed for individuals aged 55 and older and offer independent living in a social setting. Residents can enjoy amenities such as fitness centers, recreational activities, and communal dining. These communities provide a balance between independence and convenience, often including maintenance-free living, which may be appealing if you are looking to simplify your lifestyle.

In recent decades, a growing number of retirees have chosen to relocate to warmer climates. This trend, seen across many parts of the world, is driven by a combination of health, economic, and lifestyle considerations. The sunbelt regions of the United States and warmer destinations continue to attract aging populations seeking comfort, affordability, and an improved quality of life.

Warmer climates often provide relief from chronic conditions such as arthritis, asthma, or other joint and respiratory ailments that can be aggravated by cold, damp weather. Sunlight, when experienced in moderation, can boost mood and increase Vitamin D, both of which contribute to mental and physical wellness in older adults.

In addition to health benefits, lifestyle appeal plays a significant role in this movement. Warmer climates often promote a more active, outdoor-oriented lifestyle, which aligns with many retirees' goals of staying fit and socially engaged. Activities such as walking, golfing, swimming, and gardening are more easily enjoyed year-round in milder temperatures. Retirees also tend to gravitate toward coastal or desert communities that offer scenic beauty and recreational amenities tailored to older residents.

Economic factors further drive this trend. Many popular warm-weather retirement destinations have a lower cost of living compared to large urban centers or colder regions. Retirees on fixed incomes may find that their savings stretch further in places with more affordable housing, healthcare, and everyday expenses.

Moreover, retirement communities and infrastructure in warmer areas are often well-developed. States like Florida, Arizona, and Texas offer extensive retirement communities with amenities that support aging in place. These areas also typically have medical facilities and services designed to meet the needs of an older population, adding to the sense of security for those relocating.

The migration of retirees to warmer climates reflects a broader desire for a healthier, more enjoyable, and often more affordable retirement.

While the sun and lifestyle are strong attractions, retirees must carefully consider all factors, including climate risks and personal support networks, when planning such a move. Nonetheless, the trend is likely to continue as the global population ages and retirement is more about quality of life.

Income tax policies are often at the center of these relocation decisions. States like California, New York, and New Jersey impose relatively high personal income tax rates, which can significantly reduce the disposable income of retirees, especially those with pensions, Social Security benefits, or investment income. In contrast, states such as Florida, Texas, and Tennessee have no state income tax, allowing retirees to retain more of their retirement income. This difference can equate to thousands of dollars in savings each year, particularly for higher-income retirees or those relying on taxable retirement accounts.

Beyond income taxes, property taxes and sales taxes are also factors in financial calculations. For example, a retiree selling a home in a high-property-tax state like Illinois may relocate to a state with more favorable property tax rates and lower housing costs, thereby reducing monthly expenses. Additionally, some states offer generous homestead exemptions or senior property tax relief programs, which further incentivize relocation for retirees on fixed budgets.

Estate taxes and inheritance taxes also influence decisions, particularly among wealthier retirees who may be concerned with passing on assets. States such as Florida and Arizona not only avoid income tax but also lack estate or inheritance taxes, making them attractive options for those seeking to preserve family wealth.

However, it is important to note that non-financial factors also play a role in relocation decisions. Access to quality healthcare, proximity to family, climate, and lifestyle preferences may outweigh tax advantages for some. Additionally, moving itself incurs costs, and the long-term benefits of lower taxes must be weighed against relocation expenses and the potential changes in community support networks.

Over recent years in the United States, there has been a noticeable shift in the housing choices of older adults (often defined as aged 65 and over), with more seniors selling their homes, downsizing, or opting for rental housing rather than continuing full homeownership. This shift reflects changing financial, demographic, and lifestyle pressures and has implications for housing markets, public policy, and retirement planning.[27]

Data demonstrates that renting among seniors has increased significantly. Between 2013 and 2023, the number of renters aged 65 and older grew by approximately 2.4 million, representing nearly a 30% increase, the largest growth of any age group in that period.[28]

This reflects a rising proportion of the senior population moving away from exclusive homeownership toward renting.[29]

In specific communities and metro areas, the shift is particularly pronounced. For example:

In Florida, senior renters increased by about 22.4% in the Miami–Fort Lauderdale–West Palm Beach metro from 2013 to 2023, for those 65+; Jacksonville saw over an 80% increase in senior renters over the same decade.[30]

Cities like Austin, Texas, recorded an 81.1% jump in renters aged 65+ in the 2013–2023 period.[31]

Several interlinked factors are driving this trend among seniors:

---

27 Homes analysis: renters aged 65+ increased by about 2.4 million between 2013 and 2023.

28 Homes analysis: renters aged 65+ increased by about 2.4 million between 2013 and 2023.

29 Homes analysis: renters aged 65+ increased by about 2.4 million between 2013 and 2023.

30 Data from the U.S. Census Bureau's American Community Survey (2013–2023).

31 U.S. Census data compiled by Point2Homes.

FINANCIAL CONSIDERATIONS AND COST OF OWNERSHIP

Owning a home involves not only mortgage costs (if applicable) but also maintenance, property taxes, insurance, and repair expenses. As homes age, upkeep becomes more demanding and costly. For many seniors living on fixed incomes or looking to free up equity, selling a home and renting can reduce financial burdens. Rising property taxes and insurance premiums are often cited as reasons for preferring rentals.[32]

DESIRE FOR FLEXIBILITY AND REDUCED RESPONSIBILITY

Renting allows older adults to avoid many of the physical and managerial responsibilities of homeownership, such as maintaining the home, lawn, roof, or dealing with large repairs. Downsizing or renting similarly may make it easier to move closer to family, access amenities, or relocate seasonally.

LIFESTYLE AND SOCIAL MOTIVATIONS

Some seniors prefer living in rental or senior housing options that offer services, social opportunities, and facilities (e.g., independent living or active-adult communities) that align with lifestyle preferences. These factors tend to be less common in traditional singlefamily homeownership.[33]

32 Joint Center for Housing Studies of Harvard University, The State of the Nation's Housing 2023.

33 *Baby Boomers Begin Making the Move to Senior Housing and Active Adult*, National Investment Center for Seniors Housing & Care.

BROADER DEMOGRAPHIC AND HOUSING MARKET TRENDS

The U.S. population is aging, and many homes owned by seniors are older, larger, and more costly to maintain. Rising housing prices and less affordability for buying or moving sometimes make renting the more practical alternative. Additionally, interest rates and credit market conditions may make purchasing or replacing a home difficult.[34]

Barriers to seniors renting include rent instability (rent increases over time), limited availability of rental housing suitable for older adults (e.g., accessible housing, onestory, or adapted units), potential pet limitations, inability to customize one's living space, and/or tenure security. Also, rents in many locations are rising rapidly, sometimes offsetting expected savings.[35]

As retirees look for ways to supplement fixed incomes (pensions, Social Security, savings), rental property ownership has featured in the mix of possible income-generating avenues. For some, owning one or more rental properties provides monthly cash flow, potential tax benefits, and equity appreciation. For others, the costs, risks, and management demands make it less feasible. Understanding how prevalent this strategy is, its benefits and drawbacks, and how trends are evolving helps to assess whether it's a practical option for many retirees.

OWNING RENTAL PROPERTIES

If managed well, rental properties can provide monthly or periodic cash flow, which helps offset living expenses, especially after retirement when employment income drops. Rents often tend to increase (though not always on an expected trajectory), which can help keep pace with

34 *America's Housing Market Is Failing Older Adults*, Urban Institute, Urban Wire, March 12, 2023.

35 *America's Housing Market Is Failing Older Adults*, Urban Institute.

inflation. Additionally, property values may be appreciated over time, adding to your wealth.

Retirees with rental properties can generally deduct maintenance, property taxes, mortgage interest (if still carrying debt), insurance, and depreciation. These deductions can reduce taxable income. Some retirees may have purchased property earlier or own homes they can turn into rentals, thereby leveraging past property investments to generate ongoing returns.

DISADVANTAGES

Even a single rental property has ongoing costs: repairs, maintenance, property management (if outsourced), insurance, and occasional major capital expenditures (roof, HVAC, etc.).

There can be periods without tenants, which means no income, while costs (taxes, insurance, and utilities, where applicable) still accrue. Dealing with problem tenants, evictions, or property damage can consume time, effort, and money.

If the retiree still has a mortgage on the rental, debt service reduces net income and adds risk. Interest rates, property tax increases, and insurance premiums can change unfavorably.

Holding too much wealth in one or a few properties also concentrates on risk. Unlike stocks or bonds, real estate is less liquid: selling a property may involve time, transaction costs, and taxes. Selling a rental property triggers capital gains taxes; depreciation recapture can impose additional tax burdens. For retirees with limited income, increases in gross income from rental operations could affect the taxation of Social Security benefits or Medicare premiums.

I'm sure you can appreciate that owning, renting, or entering independent living requires a careful decision-making process. Children, grandchildren, and other family members' needs must be taken into consideration.

There is yet another option. I call it the "Tom Selleck" option of a reverse mortgage.

A reverse mortgage is a financial product designed primarily for homeowners aged 62 or older, allowing them to convert part of their home's equity into cash while continuing to live in the property. Unlike a traditional mortgage, where the borrower makes monthly payments to the lender, in a reverse mortgage, the lender makes loan payments to the homeowner. The loan balance grows over time as interest and fees accumulate, and repayment is typically deferred until the homeowner sells the home, moves out permanently, or passes away.

The most common type of reverse mortgage is the Home Equity Conversion Mortgage, also known as HECM, which is insured by the Federal Housing Administration, or FHA. In this scenario, the homeowner remains responsible for property taxes, homeowners' insurance, and maintenance of the property. Loan proceeds can be received as a lump sum, in monthly payments, through a line of credit, or via a combination of these options.

One of the main advantages of a reverse mortgage is that it provides retirees with additional income, helping to supplement Social Security or pension benefits. This can be especially useful for those with limited savings or fixed incomes. Another benefit is that there are no required monthly mortgage payments, reducing financial pressure. Homeowners retain ownership and can continue living in their homes if they meet the loan terms. Additionally, since reverse mortgages are non-recourse loans, borrowers or their heirs will never owe more than the home's value when the loan is repaid.

However, reverse mortgages also have drawbacks. The loan balance increases over time, which means the homeowner's equity decreases as interest and fees accumulate. This can reduce the inheritance left to heirs. The costs associated with reverse mortgages, such as origination fees, insurance premiums, and interest, can also be higher than those of traditional home loans. If the homeowner fails to pay property taxes, insurance, or maintain the home, the lender can foreclose. Moreover, if the homeowner moves out or passes away, the loan becomes due, potentially forcing heirs to sell the property to repay the debt.

A reverse mortgage can be a valuable tool for older homeowners seeking financial flexibility and security during retirement. However, it is not suitable for everyone. Careful considerations of long-term goals, cost, and family implications are essential before deciding if a reverse mortgage is the right choice.

As a New Jersey loan originator, I do not recommend a reverse mortgage unless the homeowner has no heirs and has little or no options to access cash. It is a complex process and understanding it can be daunting.

My client, Mary, chose to transfer the deed of her home to her youngest daughter based on the guidance of an elder law attorney. While transferring property to children or into a trust can provide certain benefits, it is important to be aware that there can also be unintended consequences, including the potential loss of valuable tax advantages. I recommend that anyone considering such a transfer consult with a CPA or qualified tax professional to fully understand the implications and ensure the decision aligns with their overall financial and estate planning goals.

Whether you choose to sell your home, move into an over-55 community, or rent an apartment, it's important to decide with your family's proximity and support in mind. Being close to family members can provide emotional comfort, social connection, and practical assistance as your needs evolve. Proximity allows for more frequent visits, shared experiences, and peace of mind knowing that help is nearby if needed.

Ultimately, where you decide to live should enhance your quality of life, not only in terms of comfort and convenience but also by maintaining strong relationships with those who matter most.

My partner and I feel truly blessed to have twelve wonderful grandchildren, all living in the Northeast. Maintaining a close connection with them is especially important to us, and we treasure the time we spend together. At the same time, we deeply appreciate the chance to enjoy Florida's west coast, where the warm, sunny winters provide a welcome contrast to the colder months up north. This seasonal flexibility allows us to balance our family commitments with a comfortable and healthy lifestyle, giving us the best of both worlds: meaningful family moments and the enjoyment of a relaxing, sun-filled environment.

"Your retirement plan has two steps: First, move somewhere that doesn't require shoveling. Step two: Forget what a snow shovel even looks like."

—Leonard Snart in The Flash, played by Wentworth Miller

CHAPTER 8

Retirement Planning 101: Building a Secure Future

Retirement planning doesn't begin with numbers; it begins with a moment.

I often ask clients to pause and picture a day in their future when the alarm clock no longer dictates their schedule. There's no rush to get out the door, no deadlines waiting. Instead, there's a choice. Maybe it's a quiet morning with coffee on the patio, the sun rising gently. Or perhaps it's boarding a plane to somewhere you've always wanted to visit. For others, it's being closer to family, attending grandchildren's events, or giving back through volunteering.

That vision, that feeling, is where retirement planning truly starts.

Behind the scenes, of course, there's a practical side. Retirement is the phase of life when your paycheck from work is replaced by the income you've built over the years, your savings, your investments, and other income sources. The goal is simple, but powerful: to ensure that the life you've imagined can be lived comfortably and confidently.

A well-structured retirement plan does more than organize finances. It provides a sense of security, knowing that your future is not left to chance. It creates independence, allowing you to make choices based on what you want, not what you have to do. And perhaps most importantly, it brings peace of mind, because you've taken the time to prepare.

But it all starts with clarity.

What does your retirement look like? Is it filled with travel and adventure? A move to a warmer climate? More time with family? Or a slower, more intentional pace of life?

Once that picture becomes clear, it becomes much easier to determine what it will take to support it. Your goals become the foundation, guiding how much income you'll need and how to build toward it over time.

In the end, retirement planning isn't just about money. It's about designing the life you want to live and making sure you have the means to enjoy it fully.

As the vision of retirement begins to take shape, the next question naturally follows: *Where will the income come from to support it?*

I would like to describe retirement income as a collection of streams rather than a single source. Imagine standing beside a calm river that's fed by several smaller streams. Each one plays a role, and together, they create a steady, reliable flow.

For most people, one of those streams begins with Social Security Administration benefits. It's a foundational piece, predictable, consistent, and designed to provide a base level of income.

Then there may be a pension, perhaps from years of service with an employer. For those fortunate enough to have one, it can feel like a paycheck that never stopped, quietly arriving each month, offering stability and reassurance.

Alongside that are the assets you've built over time, retirement accounts like 401(k)s and IRAs, as well as personal investment portfolios. These are often the result of decades of discipline, saving, and thoughtful planning. Unlike the fixed streams, these require a bit more attention, deciding when and how much to draw, ensuring they last as long as you do.

And sometimes, retirement doesn't mean a complete stop. For many, it includes a new chapter, consulting, part-time work, or pursuing something they simply enjoy that also generates income. Not out of necessity, but out of purpose.

The key is not relying too heavily on any one stream but rather creating balance among them. When properly aligned, these sources work together to provide a steady, sustainable cash flow, one that supports your lifestyle without constant worry.

Because in the end, retirement isn't just about having income, it's about having confidence that no matter what lies ahead, the flow will continue.

I often tell people to imagine planting a tree. In the early years, it didn't look like just a small sapling in the ground. But beneath the surface, something powerful is happening. With time, sunlight, and care, it begins to grow. Slowly at first, then more noticeably, until one day it stands tall and strong.

That's the power of compounding.

Compound Interest is what turns modest, consistent contributions into something meaningful over time. The earlier you begin, the more time your money has to grow—not just from what you put in, but from what it earns along the way. In fact, those early dollars often become the most valuable ones you'll ever invest.

But saving alone isn't enough. How that money is invested plays an equally important role in shaping the outcome.

Think of investing as building a well-balanced structure. You wouldn't rely on a single pillar to hold everything up. Instead, you spread the weight across different supports—each serving a purpose.

A diversified approach, spreading assets across stocks, bonds, and cash equivalents, helps create that balance. Stocks offer growth and opportunity. Bonds provide stability and income. Cash equivalents bring liquidity and safety. Together, they work in harmony, helping manage risk while still allowing your money to potentially grow.

The mix of those investments naturally evolves. When you're younger, with years ahead of you, there's more room to lean into growth, often with a higher allocation to stocks. As retirement approaches, the focus gradually shifts from building wealth to protecting it. The structure becomes more conservative, designed to weather uncertainty and preserve what you've worked so hard to accumulate.

In the end, it's not about chasing the highest return or timing the market perfectly. It's about consistency, patience, and thoughtful balance.

Because just like that tree, given enough time and the right care, what starts small can grow into something remarkably strong.

There's a part of retirement planning that many people prefer not to think about, but it's one of the most important conversations you can have.

I've sat with countless individuals who have done everything right, saved diligently, invested wisely, and built a meaningful nest egg. Yet, when the topic of healthcare comes up, there's often a pause. Not out of confusion, but hesitation. It's simply not an easy subject.

But the reality is, as we move into later years, healthcare becomes a central part of the retirement journey. I like to frame it this way: if your retirement plan is designed to create freedom, then healthcare planning is what helps protect it.

Programs like Medicare provide an essential foundation, helping cover many medical expenses. However, they don't cover everything. That's where supplemental policies and long-term care insurance come into play—filling in the gaps and preparing for scenarios that could otherwise place a significant strain on your finances.

Because the truth is, medical expenses can rise quickly and unexpectedly. Whether it's a sudden illness or the need for extended care, these moments can challenge even the most well-prepared financial plan.

But with thoughtful planning, those challenges don't have to become burdens.

By putting the right protections in place, you help preserve the assets you've worked so hard to build. More importantly, you reduce the emotional and financial stress that often accompanies health-related events, allowing you and your family to focus on care and quality of life, rather than cost.

This is why I've taken the time to discuss these topics at length in previous chapters. Not to overwhelm, but to prepare you, so you can approach this stage of life with clarity, confidence, and control.

Because retirement isn't just about enjoying the good years. It's about being ready for all of them.

As retirement comes into focus, there's another layer of planning that quietly shapes how far your money will truly go: tax efficiency.

I often explain it this way: it's not just about what you've saved, but what you get to keep.

Over the years, many people accumulate wealth across different types of accounts, such as traditional IRAs, Roth IRAs, and taxable investment portfolios. On the surface, they may look similar, but beneath it all, each one is governed by its own set of tax rules. Some will be taxed when you withdraw, others grow tax-free, and some create tax implications along the way.

The real opportunity lies in how and when you draw from them.

A thoughtful, strategic approach, whether it's coordinating withdrawals, considering Roth conversions, or leaning into tax-advantaged investments, may significantly help to manage your overall tax burden over time. Done correctly, it allows your retirement income to stretch further, without requiring you to take on additional risk.

But just as important as where you withdraw from is how much you withdraw.

This is where strategy becomes essential.

You may have heard of the 4% Rule, a widely referenced guideline suggesting that withdrawing 4% of your retirement savings each year could allow your portfolio to last for approximately 30 years. It's a helpful starting point, a framework that brings structure to an otherwise complex decision.

But retirement isn't lived on paper.

Markets shift. Inflation rises and falls. Life unfolds in ways we can't always predict. Because of that, no single rule should be followed blindly. The most effective withdrawal strategies are flexible, adjusting over time based on performance, economic conditions, and personal needs.

In the end, tax planning and withdrawal strategy work hand in hand. Together, they help ensure that your resources are used wisely, preserved thoughtfully, and aligned with the life you've worked so hard to build.

Because retirement isn't just about having enough, it's about making it last.

"Retirement planning is more than saving money; it's a lifelong process of setting goals, managing resources, and preparing for future uncertainties."

—Mario Sicari AIF CLU ChFC CLF

When you start early, invest wisely, and review plans regularly, you can enjoy a comfortable and secure retirement, free from unnecessary financial worry.

GETTING STARTED

The first step in preparing for retirement is gently taking stock of all your potential income sources. This includes Social Security Administration benefits, pensions, retirement accounts like 401(k)s and IRAs, investment portfolios, and any part-time work you might consider.

By understanding when each source will begin paying out and roughly how much it will provide, you can begin to see the bigger picture of the resources available to support your desired lifestyle. For couples, this step can be especially helpful in coordinating the timing of benefits, such as Social Security, which can make a meaningful difference in household income while also taking longevity and tax considerations into account.

It's less about creating pressure and more about gaining clarity and confidence, so you can approach retirement with a sense of ease and control.

The next step is to take a thoughtful look at your current expenses and anticipate what your future needs might be. Start by creating a clear, detailed budget, separating essential costs like housing, utilities, groceries, insurance, and healthcare from discretionary spending, such as travel, hobbies, and entertainment. Planning for inflation and unexpected events, like medical emergencies, helps ensure that your savings will continue to support your lifestyle comfortably over time. For couples, open conversations about lifestyle expectations are especially important, since differing priorities can influence both spending and savings decisions.

It's also important not to overlook debts and other financial obligations. Entering retirement with high-interest debt can quietly erode your savings and add unnecessary stress. Paying down consumer debt, such as credit cards or personal loans, before retiring is often a wise approach. Mortgage considerations deserve careful attention as well. A mortgage-free home can significantly reduce monthly expenses and offer greater flexibility in how and where you choose to live during retirement.

By taking the time to evaluate both expenses and liabilities now, you set the stage for a retirement that feels secure, manageable, and aligned with the lifestyle you hope to enjoy.

Understanding how your investments and retirement accounts are allocated becomes more than just a numbers game; it becomes part of the story of your future. Over time, most people find their comfort with risk changes. What once felt exciting may now feel uncertain, and it becomes important to adjust investment strategies to reflect that shift. This often means dialing back exposure to highly volatile assets, while keeping enough growth-oriented investments to ensure your money can support you over the long haul.

For couples, this process takes on an added layer of collaboration. Reviewing portfolios together allows both partners to see the full picture, ensure diversification, and find a balance that respects each person's comfort with risk and their shared timeline for retirement. It's not just about math; it's about building confidence in the life you envision together.

In my first book, *The Art of Creating Wealth,* I likened budgeting to laying the foundation for a house. It is the sturdy base upon which saving and investing can grow. But even with a solid foundation, discernment is essential. It's easy to be tempted by designer clothing, luxury cars, or extravagant vacations, but these pleasures come with a cost. When viewed through the lens of long-term financial security, it becomes clear which desires are sustainable and which might threaten the plans you've worked so hard to build.

Retirement planning, in the end, is as much about choices as it is about numbers. It's about carefully weighing what truly matters, aligning your resources with your vision, and making each financial decision a stepping-stone toward the future you want to live.

Even if you've reached a point of significant financial success, with the freedom to enjoy the rewards of your hard work, it's important to remember that this doesn't come with a guaranteed paycheck or a steady income stream. In retirement, your lifestyle will likely rely on a mix of investments, pension payments, and Social Security.

Yet not all expenses are predictable. Taxes can fluctuate with changes in income, property assessments, or new legislation, while everyday necessities, like groceries, utilities, and healthcare, may rise over time due to inflation or local market shifts.

By keeping in mind that these essential costs are not fixed, you gain the ability to plan more realistically. This awareness helps protect your financial stability, reduces stress, and ensures your resources will continue to support the life you've worked to build, without unwelcome surprises along the way.

"Retirement is wonderful if you have two essentials: much to live on and much to live for."

—Unknown

CHAPTER 9

Annuities In Retirement

As you approach retirement, one of the greatest financial challenges you may face is ensuring a steady and reliable income for the rest of your life. While savings accounts, pensions, and investment portfolios can provide income, many retirees seek an additional layer of financial security that guarantees consistent payments regardless of market fluctuations or lifespan. This is where annuities can play a significant role.

An annuity is a financial product offered by insurance companies designed to provide a stream of income, typically for life, in exchange for an upfront deposit. Essentially, an individual pays a lump sum or a series of payments to an insurance company, which in turn promises to make regular payments back to the individual either immediately or at some point in the future. The main purpose of an annuity in retirement is to create a predictable source of income, supplementing other retirement income sources such as Social Security, pensions, and personal savings.

Think of the lottery; winners are often given two choices: a lump-sum cash payment or an annuity. In many cases, the advertised jackpot represents the annuity value, which is the total amount that would be paid out over time. The cash option, however, is usually much lower because it reflects the present value of that future stream of payments. In other words, the lump-sum payment represents the discounted value of the annuity, the amount that would need to be invested today to generate the same income over time.

Insurance companies have developed a wide range of annuity products, each designed to meet different financial goals. It is important to understand how these various features work and how they can fit into and enhance your overall retirement plan.

Let's discuss the different types of annuities available in the marketplace.

Fixed annuities are the most straightforward type of annuity. They offer a guaranteed rate of return for a specified period and predictable income payments. The insurance company assumes all investment risk, making this option ideal for conservative investors who prioritize stability over risk of losses. Payments can be structured to last for a certain number of years or for the lifetime of the annuity. Because the return is fixed, retirees can easily plan their budgets without worrying about market volatility.

Another variation, and a bit more complex, is variable annuities. These contracts allow investors to allocate their funds among a selection of investment subaccounts, which function similarly to mutual funds. The income and account value fluctuate based on the performance of these investments. This type of annuity provides growth potential but also involves market risk, meaning the income stream is not guaranteed. To offset this, some variable annuities include optional riders that guarantee minimum income levels or death benefits for an added cost.

Indexed annuities (also known as fixed-index annuities) blend characteristics of both fixed and variable annuities. Returns are linked to the performance of a market index, such as the S&P 500, but they also include a guaranteed minimum interest rate to protect against market downturns. Gains are typically capped or subject to participation rates, which limit how much of the market's growth is credited to the account. These annuities appeal to individuals seeking moderate growth potential with a level of downside protection.

An immediate annuity begins paying income almost right after a lump-sum payment is made, typically within 12 months. Retirees often use this product to turn a portion of their savings into guaranteed income right at the start of retirement. The payments can be set for a fixed term or for life, providing a simple and reliable income solution. Immediate annuities are particularly attractive for those who prioritize guaranteed cash flow and longevity protection.

Unlike immediate annuities, deferred annuities begin income payments at a later date, allowing the invested funds to grow tax-deferred in the interim. Deferred annuities are often used by people who are still working or are not yet ready to draw income. They provide flexibility in determining when payments begin, which can help optimize tax efficiency and long-term retirement planning.

SUITABILITY AND DISCLOSURE RULES FOR ANNUITY SALES: ENSURING RESPONSIBLE RETIREMENT PLANNING

Annuities can be valuable tools for retirement planning, offering guaranteed income, tax-deferred growth, and protection against longevity risk. However, because these products are complex financial instruments, regulators have established strict rules to ensure that annuities are sold appropriately and that prospective buyers fully understand the costs, benefits, and risks involved. Central to these rules are suitability standards and disclosure requirements, both of which aim to protect consumers and promote responsible financial decision-making.

Suitability rules require financial professionals to recommend products that are appropriate for the client's financial situation, objectives, and risk tolerance. In other words, an annuity should not be sold simply because it generates a commission for the salesperson; it must meet the specific needs of the individual investor. Factors that brokers and insurance agents must consider include the client's age, investment time horizon, liquidity needs, income requirements, financial goals, and experience with similar financial products.

For instance, selling a variable annuity with significant market risk to a retiree who prioritizes capital preservation would likely violate suitability standards. Likewise, recommending a deferred annuity to an investor who needs immediate income would be inappropriate. Suitability rules also extend to the evaluation of specific annuity features, such as surrender charges, riders, and payout options. By ensuring that the product aligns with the client's objectives, these rules protect consumers from unsuitable investments that could jeopardize their financial security.

Annuities often come with multiple layers of fees, which can include front-end sales loads, surrender charges, administrative fees, mortality and expense (M&E) risk charges, and investment management fees for subaccounts in variable annuities. Transparency regarding these costs is critical because fees directly impact the long-term growth of the annuity and the income it will generate during retirement.

Regulators require that insurers and financial professionals provide clear, comprehensive disclosures of all fees and charges associated with an annuity before a sale is completed. These disclosures must outline the cost of optional features or riders, the schedule of surrender charges, and any limitations on withdrawals. Additionally, consumers should be informed about how fees affect the projected accumulation value and payout amounts of the annuity. By providing this information, prospective buyers can make informed decisions and compare products accurately, preventing surprises that may compromise retirement planning.

Multiple regulatory bodies oversee annuity sales to enforce suitability and disclosure standards. In the United States, the Financial Industry Regulatory Authority (FINRA) sets rules for broker-dealers, while state insurance departments regulate agents and insurance companies. FINRA's rules, such as Rule 2111, require firms and registered representatives to have a reasonable basis to believe a recommended annuity is suitable for a client, considering the client's financial profile.

Best practices for compliance go beyond regulatory requirements. Financial professionals are encouraged to conduct thorough fact-finding interviews, document the rationale for their recommendations, provide clients with illustrative examples of projected costs and payouts, and offer plain-language explanations of complex terms. These practices build trust, reduce the risk of disputes, and ensure that annuities truly serve consumers' retirement needs. By ensuring that products are appropriate for the client and that all fees and charges are transparently communicated, these rules protect consumers and promote confidence in the retirement planning process. For these reasons, both consumers and financial professionals must prioritize clarity, transparency, and careful consideration when engaging in annuity transactions.

Disclosure:

Fixed and Variable annuities are suitable for long-term investing, such as retirement investing. Gains from tax-deferred investments are taxable as ordinary income upon withdrawal. Guarantees are based on the claims paying ability of the issuing company. Withdrawals made prior to age 59 ½ are subject to a 10% IRS penalty tax and surrender charges may apply. Variable annuities are subject to market risk and may lose value.

Fixed Indexed Annuities (FIA) are not suitable for all investors. FIAs permit investors to participate in only a stated percentage of an increase in an index (participation rate) and may impose a maximum annual account value percentage increase. FIAs typically do not allow for participation in dividends accumulated on the securities represented by the index.

Riders are additional guarantee options that are available to an annuity or life insurance contract holder. While some riders are part of an existing contract, many others may carry additional fees, charges and restrictions, and the policy holder should review their contract carefully before purchasing. Guarantees are based on the claims paying ability of the issuing insurance company.

It is important for me to stress to you the significance of a clear and concise understanding of these products. When serving in my capacity as an Investment Advisor, I act as a fiduciary; I recognize that conflicts of interest and sales incentives can sometimes result in recommendations that are not in the client's best interest. Throughout my career, I have seen many instances where these products were used in ways that did not benefit the owner. That said, there are circumstances in which these products can address specific needs and, when used appropriately, should be carefully considered as part of a comprehensive financial plan.

Flor had spent a lifetime caring for others, but at 80 years old, life had narrowed into a quieter, more fragile routine. Her husband, strong and independent, was now confined to a wheelchair, relying on her for nearly everything. Every decision she made carried weight, not just for herself, but for both.

Like many in her position, Flor wanted safety. Stability. A place where their savings could rest without worry. But the rates offered by her local banks left her uneasy, too low to keep up with the rising cost of living, too limiting for what she knew they might need.

So, when a family friend suggested speaking with her son, a broker, it felt like a fortunate connection. Someone she could trust. Someone who would look out for her.

The recommendation came quickly, moving her husband's assets into a non-qualified variable annuity. It was presented as a solution, something more sophisticated, something better. Trusting the relationship and the guidance, Flor agreed.

Calls went unanswered. Questions lingered. What had once felt like a step forward slowly became a source of confusion and concern. Flor didn't fully understand what she owned, only that she no longer felt in control.

That's when she reached out to me.

She had discovered that our firm served as custodians for some of their smaller accounts, and she was searching, not just for answers, but for clarity, for someone to simply explain what had been done.

As I sat with Flor and carefully reviewed their holdings, including the variable annuity contract, a difficult reality began to emerge. The product was complex. The circumstances surrounding its purchase raised concerns. Yet from a regulatory and contractual standpoint, unwinding or proving the sale should never have happened would be an uphill battle.

It was no longer about what should have been done, but what could be done now. It was about restoring her confidence, simplifying what had become complicated, and helping her regain a sense of control in a chapter of life where peace of mind matters most.

Flor didn't need sophistication. She needed transparency. She needed guidance. She needed someone in her corner.

One of the key features of annuities is that they grow on a tax-deferred basis. Unlike traditional investment accounts, where interest, dividends, and capital gains may be taxed annually, annuity earnings are not subject to income tax until withdrawals are made. This allows the investment to compound more efficiently over time, as earnings are reinvested without the drag of annual taxation. For example, interest earned in a fixed annuity or gains from a variable annuity subaccount accumulate without immediate taxation, potentially increasing the overall value of the investment.

When funds are withdrawn from an annuity, they are subject to taxation based on the type of contribution and the form of withdrawal. For non-qualified annuities purchased with after-tax dollars, only the earnings portion of a withdrawal is taxed as ordinary income. The original principal, or the amount invested, is not taxed again since it was funded with after-tax dollars. In contrast, qualified annuities purchased within retirement accounts such as IRAs or 401(k)s are funded with pretax dollars. Whereas withdrawals from these accounts are fully taxable as ordinary income, including both the principal and any accumulated earnings.

Annuities also carry penalties for early withdrawals. Generally, withdrawals made before age 59½ are subject to a 10% federal early withdrawal penalty in addition to regular income taxes, like other retirement accounts. Some exceptions exist, such as withdrawals due to disability, death, or specific annuity features you may be able to take advantage of, like periodic payments or substantially equal periodic distributions. It is important for investors to understand these rules to avoid unexpected penalties and preserve retirement savings.

When an annuity is annuitized, in other words, converted into a stream of periodic income payments, the taxation depends on whether the annuity is qualified or non-qualified. For non-qualified annuities, each payment is typically divided between a return of principal (which is tax-free) and earnings (which are taxable). Over time, the tax-free portion gradually decreases as more of the earnings are included in the payments. All payments are taxed as ordinary income in qualified annuities because both contributions and earnings have not been previously taxed.

If the owner of an annuity dies, the tax treatment of the death benefit also varies. For non-qualified annuities, beneficiaries generally owe income tax on the earnings portion of the benefit, while the principal is not taxed. Inherited qualified annuities are fully taxable as ordinary income. Certain estate planning strategies, such as stretching distributions over the beneficiary's lifetime or using lump-sum payments, can influence the tax impact and should be considered carefully.

If there's one piece of advice I would share from experience, it's this: slow down and utterly understand what you're buying, especially when it comes to complex insurance products.

These aren't simple, one-layer decisions. They often come with multiple moving parts, fees, features, and restrictions, all working together in ways that aren't always obvious at first glance. What may sound like a great solution upfront can carry long-term implications that only become clear later.

Take the time to read through everything carefully. Ask questions, then ask a few more. And don't hesitate to bring in a trusted financial advisor or insurance professional who can walk you through it in plain terms.

At the end of the day, this isn't just about making a purchase; it's about making sure the decision truly supports your goals and doesn't create unintended surprises down the road.

Many people mistakenly see them as a tool for tax avoidance, but that is not the case. Ultimately, the proceeds from the annuity will be subject to taxation. Upon the death of the annuitant, the earnings portion of the annuity is taxed as ordinary income, rather than benefiting from a step-up in basis, which adjusts the value of most inherited assets to their date-of-death value.

Here's a simple explanation of the tax liability for a non-qualified annuity:

Suppose someone purchases a non-qualified annuity for $500,000, and over 10 years, it grows to $1,000,000. The growth of $500,000 represents taxable earnings, while the original $500,000 principal was already funded with after-tax dollars.

- Taxable portion: $1,000,000 (value at withdrawal) – $500,000 (principal) = $500,000 in earnings
- Tax treatment: The $500,000 in earnings is taxed as ordinary income when withdrawn, not at capital gains rates.
- Example: If the annuitant is in the 24% federal income tax bracket, the tax on the earnings would be approximately $500,000 × 24% = $120,000.

This tax would be assessed to the beneficiary as income in respect to the decedent.

Here's a simple explanation of the tax liability for an individual stock held until death:

Assume an individual purchases stock for $500,000, and over 10 years, it grows to $1,000,000. If the stock is held until the owner's death, the tax treatment is different from an annuity because of the step-up in basis rules.

- Step-up in basis: At death, the cost basis of the stock is adjusted to its fair market value on the date of death. In this example, the basis steps up from $500,000 to $1,000,000.
- Taxable gain: Because the basis is now $1,000,000, there is no capital gain for the heirs on this appreciation. If the heirs sell the stock immediately at the stepped-up value, they will owe no capital gains tax.
- Key difference from an annuity: Unlike a non-qualified annuity, which taxes the earnings as ordinary income to the beneficiary, inherited stock benefits from the step-up basis, eliminating the unrealized capital gains for tax purposes.

This illustrates why other asset classes and other inherited assets can be more tax-efficient than non-qualified annuities when passed to heirs.

Individuals who own annuities are offered options when it comes to receiving their income payments. These options allow people to tailor their income to meet personal financial needs, manage longevity risk, and address estate planning considerations. Understanding these choices is essential for making informed decisions about retirement income.

LIFE INCOME OPTION

A life-only annuity provides income payments for the lifetime of the annuitant. Payments cease upon the annuitant's death, meaning no residual value is paid to beneficiaries. This option typically offers the highest monthly payment because the insurance company's obligation ends with the annuitant's life, and no additional risk is assumed for beneficiaries.

LIFE WITH PERIOD CERTAIN

This option guarantees income for the lifetime of the annuitant but also includes a minimum guaranteed period, such as 10 or 20 years. If the annuitant dies before the period ends, the remaining payments continue to a designated beneficiary, providing a balance between lifetime income and protection for heirs, though monthly payments are lower than a life-only annuity due to the additional risk assumed by the insurer.

JOINT AND SURVIVOR ANNUITY

A joint and survivor annuity is designed for two individuals, typically spouses. Income continues for the lifetime of the surviving individual after the death of the first annuitant. The payments are often reduced compared to a single-life annuity because the insurance company is making payments over a longer potential period. Variations include partial survivor payments, such as 50%, 66%, or 100% of the original amount.

FIXED PERIOD ANNUITY

Also called a "period-certain annuity," this option guarantees payments for a specific number of years, regardless of whether the annuitant lives or dies. While it does not provide a lifetime income, it ensures predictable cash flow for the chosen period. Fixed-period annuities are often used for short-term income needs or to bridge the gap until other retirement income sources begin.

LUMP SUM WITHDRAWAL

Although technically not an annuitization option, some annuities allow the owner to take the entire value as a lump sum. While convenient, this approach forfeits the guarantees of periodic payments and can trigger significant tax consequences, as the earnings portion is taxed as ordinary income. Additionally, withdrawals before age 59½ may be subject to a 10% early withdrawal penalty.

SYSTEMATIC WITHDRAWAL

Many annuities allow for scheduled withdrawals over time without formal annuitization. The annuitant can receive regular distributions while leaving the remaining balance invested. This option provides flexibility and potential growth but typically does not guarantee lifetime income unless the annuity is eventually converted to a life or joint-life payout.

Let's analyze the single premium immediate annuity, also known as SPIA. This is a type of annuity designed to provide a guaranteed stream of income almost immediately after a lump sum payment is made. SPIAs are often used by retirees who want to convert a portion of their savings into a predictable income that can supplement Social

Security, pensions, or other retirement resources. These annuities are particularly appealing if you want financial stability and protection against the risk of outliving your savings.

An SPIA is purchased with a single, upfront premium, typically from the retiree's savings or investment account. In exchange for this lump-sum payment, the insurance company guarantees a series of regular payments that begin shortly after the purchase, usually within a month to a year. The amount of the payment depends on several factors, including the size of the premium, the age and gender of the annuitant, the payment frequency, and any optional features such as cost-of-living adjustments or survivor benefits.

SPIAs purchased with non-qualified funds (after-tax dollars) grow tax-deferred, and only the earnings portion of each payment is taxed as ordinary income. The return of principal is not taxed again. For qualified funds (e.g., IRA or 401(k) funds), all payments are fully taxable as ordinary income because both contributions and earnings were not previously taxed. Understanding the tax implications is crucial when planning the size and timing of SPIA payments.

ADVANTAGES OF AN SPIA

1. Predictable Income: SPIAs provide a guaranteed, regular income stream that can help cover essential expenses in retirement.
2. Longevity Protection: Life-only or joint-life options protect against the risk of outliving savings.
3. Simplicity: Once purchased, SPIA requires minimal ongoing management, allowing retirees to focus on other aspects of retirement planning.

While SPIAs offer many benefits, there are trade-offs. The lump-sum premium is generally irrevocable, meaning the money cannot be accessed once the annuity is purchased, except through structured withdrawals if allowed. Additionally, inflation can erode the purchasing power of fixed payments unless a cost-of-living adjustment is included. Finally, SPIAs may not provide flexibility for heirs unless a period-certain or joint-life option is chosen.

I'd like to share a personal story that has shaped how I think about financial planning. My mother was married to a remarkably hardworking and successful man who built significant wealth through commercial real estate early in his career. Over the years, he amassed an impressive portfolio of properties. When he passed away, my mother suddenly faced the enormous responsibility of managing these assets on her own.

Although she asked for my help in carrying on my father's legacy, the task quickly proved overwhelming. Together, we made the difficult decision to liquidate the real estate and reallocate the proceeds into income-producing investments.

My mother, born in 1935 and a proud member of the Silent Generation, was exceptionally frugal, a characteristic shared by many of her peers. She was determined that a portion of the proceeds be placed into an investment that would provide her with a guaranteed stream of income for the rest of her life. After evaluating our options, we chose a Single Premium Immediate Annuity (SPIA).

This decision gave her peace of mind. The SPIA provided a reliable, lifetime income, while any remaining principal could be preserved for her beneficiaries. It was a solution that balanced security, prudence, and foresight, a reflection of the values she has carried throughout her life.

CHAPTER 10

Asset Allocation and Its Importance

Asset allocation refers to the strategic distribution of an individual's investment portfolio among various asset classes, typically stocks, bonds, and cash equivalents, to help achieve a balance between risk and return. Asset allocation does not ensure a profit or protect against a loss. It is a cornerstone of sound financial planning and becomes especially significant during retirement, a stage when preserving wealth and generating consistent income are paramount.

During one's working years, investors generally emphasize growth-oriented assets, such as equities, to maximize long-term returns. However, as retirement approaches, the focus often shifts from accumulation to preservation and income generation. This transition underscores the importance of a carefully structured asset allocation strategy that mitigates market volatility while ensuring the portfolio continues to grow enough to outpace inflation and sustain withdrawals over potentially decades of retirement life.

A critical aspect of asset allocation in retirement is the *rebalancing process.* Over time, market fluctuations can cause the proportion of assets in each class to drift from its original target. Rebalancing involves periodically adjusting the portfolio to restore the intended allocation, thereby maintaining the desired level of risk and return. This disciplined approach prevents emotional decision-making, which can lead to suboptimal results, such as selling during downturns or overinvesting in an overperforming sector.

In addition, asset allocation strategies should account for inflation and longevity risk. Retirees are living longer, and purchasing power declines over time. Thus, maintaining some exposure to equities, despite their volatility, is crucial for long-term growth potential and for preserving real wealth throughout retirement. In contrast, overly conservative portfolios that rely heavily on fixed-income investments may struggle to keep pace with inflation, jeopardizing financial security later in life.

Inflation risk has contributed to significant market fluctuations in recent years. Much of this inflation can be traced to the unintended consequences of expansive government stimulus programs and prolonged accommodative Federal Reserve policies. During periods of economic uncertainty, such as the pandemic, the federal government injected large amounts of liquidity into the economy to support growth and consumer spending. While these measures helped avoid a severe recession, they also increased the money supply, which eventually fueled higher inflation levels once demand began to exceed supply.

In response to rising inflation, the Federal Reserve then implemented a series of interest rate hikes aimed at cooling the economy and restoring price stability. However, this monetary tightening had a pronounced impact on the bond market. As interest rates increased, the market value of bonds declined, since their lower coupon payments became less attractive when compared to newly issued bonds offering higher yields. This inverse relationship between interest rates and bond prices led to heightened volatility and a decline in bond valuations across many investment portfolios.

For investors, particularly retirees or those holding fixed-income securities, the effects were substantial. Portfolios that had previously relied on bonds for stability and income experienced unexpected fluctuations and temporary losses. This period served as a reminder that even traditionally "safe" assets such as bonds carry risk, particularly in a rapidly changing interest rate environment. Consequently, investors have been encouraged to reassess their asset allocation strategies, balancing the need for income with protection against interest rate and inflation risks.

Ultimately, there is no one-size-fits-all approach to asset allocation. Factors such as risk tolerance, life expectancy, income needs, and other personal circumstances must guide the strategy. Many financial planners advocate for a "glide path" model, gradually shifting from aggressive to more conservative allocations as individuals age. This approach allows for growth during early retirement while providing stability and predictable income in later years.

One of my biggest concerns when working with retirees is whether they're truly able to set clear, objective investment goals that honestly reflect their comfort with risk.

I've seen too often how emotions can quietly take over the process. A recent market swing, a past loss, or even a period of strong returns can shape how someone *feels* about risk, rather than what's appropriate for their situation. At times, there's also a sense of overconfidence that can creep in, especially after things have gone well.

The challenge is separating those emotions from reality, stepping back and asking, "What level of risk truly fits my lifestyle, my needs, and my long-term security?" Because getting that part right is what ultimately makes everything else work.

In 2010, interest rates on traditional savings vehicles such as Certificates of Deposit (CDs) and money market accounts remained at historically low levels. This environment reflected the broader economic context following the 2008 financial crisis, when the Federal Reserve maintained an accommodative monetary policy to stimulate economic recovery. As a result, savers faced limited returns on low-risk, interest-bearing accounts, while borrowers benefited from exceptionally low lending rates.

During this period, the average yield on CDs varied by term but remained well below historical norms. According to financial data sources, the average annual percentage yield (APY) on a 1-year CD was approximately 0.70% in 2010, while a 6-month CD offered around 0.46% APY. Shorter-term CDs, such as those with a 3-month maturity, yielded roughly 0.30% APY. These figures reflected the persistent influence of near-zero federal funds rates, which limited banks' incentive to offer higher yields to attract deposits.[36]

Similarly, money market accounts and funds offered minimal returns throughout 2010. The average yield on taxable money market mutual funds hovered just above zero, reflecting the lingering effects of the Federal Reserve's target rate range of 0.00% to 0.25%.[37] For money market deposit accounts, the average rate at credit unions was about 0.54%, while banks offered slightly less, averaging around 0.31% in the first quarter of 2010.[38] These returns were consistent with the broader trend of suppressed interest income for conservative investors seeking liquidity and safety.

The low-rate environment of 2010 emphasized the trade-off between safety and return in personal finance. While CDs and money market accounts provided principal protection and liquidity, their limited yields struggled to keep pace with inflation, resulting in negligible real returns. Consequently, many investors were prompted to reconsider their asset allocation strategies, balancing the desire for security with the need for growth in an era of historically low interest rates.

Today, we see a normalization of the interest rate market. As of 2025, interest rates on traditional low-risk savings instruments such as Certificates of Deposit (CDs) and money market accounts have risen significantly compared to the historically low levels of the past decade. These changes reflect the Federal Reserve's tightening of monetary

36 *Average Bank CD Rates over the Last Ten Years*, Safe Money.

37 *Money Market Mutual Fund Assets and Trends 2010 Report*, Investment Company Institute (ICI), 2011.

38 *Credit Union and Bank Rates – 2010 Q1*, National Credit Union Administration, NCUA.gov, 2010.

policy in response to inflationary pressures, as well as increased competition among financial institutions for deposits.

Disclosure:

CDs are FDIC insured to specific limits and offer a fixed rate of return if held to maturity, whereas investing in securities is subject to market risk including loss of principal. An investment in the Fund is not insured or guaranteed by the Federal Deposit Insurance Corporation or any other government agency. Although the Fund seeks to preserve the value of your investment at $1.00 per share, it is possible to lose money by investing in the Fund.

In 2010, many retirees responded to historically low interest rates by overweighting equities in their investment portfolios, particularly through diversified exposure to dividend-paying stocks. This strategy allowed them to offset the loss of income that resulted from the minimal yields offered by traditionally safer vehicles such as CDs and money market accounts. By capturing both dividend income and potential capital appreciation, retirees were able to maintain a meaningful level of portfolio income despite the challenging low-rate environment.

Over the ensuing years, exceptional market performance further contributed to substantial growth in portfolio values. Those who maintained exposure to equities benefited from prolonged bull markets and recovering global economies, resulting in significant wealth accumulation. However, it is important to note that these same retirees are now 15 years older than they were in 2010, bringing with them increased longevity risk and potentially different income needs.

As investors age, particularly after observing the volatility inherent in both bond and stock markets, it becomes increasingly critical to mitigate risk. Understanding and implementing effective risk-management strategies is one of the most important principles for preserving capital, maintaining portfolio stability, and ensuring that retirement income needs are met over the long term.

The bucket theory is a strategic approach to investing and is particularly popular among retirees or those nearing retirement, as it is designed to balance income stability and long-term growth. The central concept involves dividing your investment portfolio into separate "buckets," each with a distinct purpose, investment horizon, and risk profile. By structuring investments in this way, you can meet your immediate financial needs while still maintaining opportunities for wealth growth over time.

THE BUCKETS

The first and most critical bucket is the short-term bucket, which typically covers the next one to three years of living expenses. This portion of the portfolio is invested in very low-risk, highly liquid assets such as cash, money market funds, or short-term bonds. The primary goal is capital preservation; retirees can rely on this bucket to meet daily expenses without the need to sell more volatile investments during unfavorable market conditions.

The second component is the medium-term bucket, usually intended to cover financial needs over the next three to ten years. Investments in this bucket often include bonds, conservative dividend-paying stocks, or balanced funds. The medium-term bucket carries a moderate level of risk, allowing for some growth while still prioritizing stability. This structure provides a buffer between immediate cash needs and long-term investments, offering flexibility in cases of unexpected expenses or market fluctuations.

The final component is the long-term bucket, which is focused on growth and typically consists of equities, equity funds, or other growth-oriented assets. Because the funds in this bucket are not needed for many years, investors can accept a higher level of risk in exchange for potential inflation-beating returns. The long-term bucket is vital for sustaining financial security in later retirement years and for leaving a legacy if desired.

The bucket theory is effective both psychologically and financially. Knowing that short-term expenses are fully covered reduces anxiety during market volatility, allowing retirees to avoid selling long-term investments at a loss. Furthermore, it provides a structured approach to portfolio management, enabling periodic rebalancing between buckets to ensure that income needs and growth objectives remain aligned over time.

Asset allocation and diversification are two foundational principles of sound investing, and while they are closely related, each serves a distinct purpose in building a resilient portfolio.

Diversification, on the other hand, focuses on reducing risk *within* each asset class by spreading your investments across a variety of individual holdings. Instead of investing solely in one stock, one bond, or one type of fund, diversification ensures that no single investment has an outsized impact on your portfolio. For example, holding a broad mix of stocks across different industries, company sizes, and geographic regions can help cushion the portfolio if one sector or region experiences a downturn. Similarly, within bonds, spreading investments across different maturities, issuers, and credit qualities helps manage interest rate and credit risks. Diversification aims to smooth returns over time by avoiding excessive concentration in any one area.

While asset allocation is the blueprint that determines how much of your portfolio goes into each major category, diversification is the technique that strengthens the structure by distributing risk within those categories.

Together, they create a balanced approach: asset allocation aligns your portfolio with your overall objectives, and diversification helps protect it from the unpredictable movement of individual investments. When used in combination, these strategies work to improve the potential for steady, long-term growth while managing the inevitable ups and downs of the market.

Many investors select multiple mutual funds based on past performance without examining the underlying holdings. While this may appear to provide diversification, it does not necessarily reduce risk. If the funds hold similar or identical investments, the portfolio experiences overlapping, which can increase risk rather than mitigate it.

The chart below displays a sample of different asset classes and the difference in performance and the level of risk associated with each classification. You will notice how, year over year, each asset class performance is different.

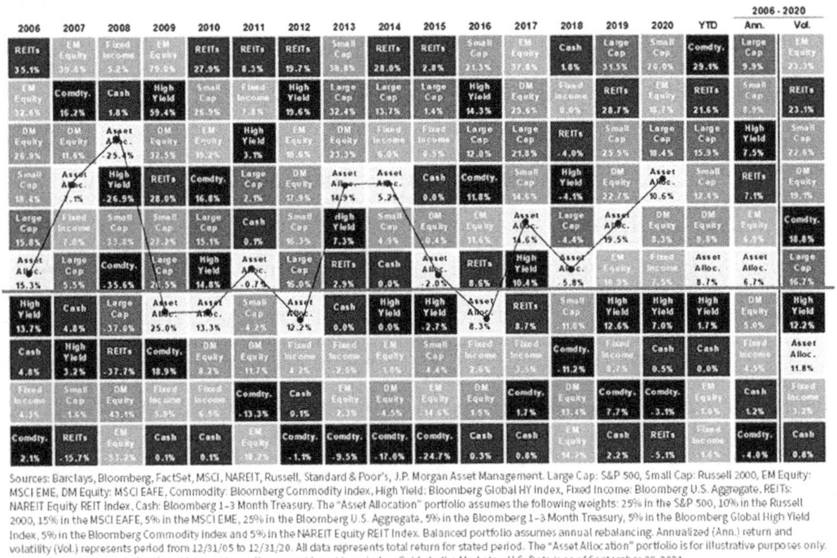

Sources: Barclays, Bloomberg, FactSet, MSCI, NAREIT, Russell, Standard & Poor's, J.P. Morgan Asset Management. Large Cap: S&P 500, Small Cap: Russell 2000, EM Equity: MSCI EME, DM Equity: MSCI EAFE, Commodity: Bloomberg Commodity Index, High Yield: Bloomberg Global HY Index, Fixed Income: Bloomberg U.S. Aggregate, REITs: NAREIT Equity REIT Index, Cash: Bloomberg 1-3 Month Treasury. The "Asset Allocation" portfolio assumes the following weights: 25% in the S&P 500, 10% in the Russell 2000, 15% in the MSCI EAFE, 5% in the MSCI EME, 25% in the Bloomberg U.S. Aggregate, 5% in the Bloomberg 1-3 Month Treasury, 5% in the Bloomberg Global High Yield Index, 5% in the Bloomberg Commodity Index and 5% in the NAREIT Equity REIT Index. Balanced portfolio assumes annual rebalancing. Annualized (Ann.) return and volatility (Vol.) represents period from 12/31/05 to 12/31/20. All data represents total return for stated period. The "Asset Allocation" portfolio is for illustrative purposes only. Past performance is not indicative of future returns. You cannot invest in an index. Guide to the Markets – U.S. Data is as of September 30, 2021.

This chart serves as a reference point, illustrating nine distinct asset classes, each with its own unique set of holdings and no overlap with the others. The white box labeled "Asset Allocation" represents a diversified mix including a percentage of each asset class. The overall risk of this allocation is driven by how much weight is assigned to higher-risk versus lower-risk categories. In this example, the portfolio reflects a 60% equity and 40% fixed-income blend.

I've found that increasingly, my client meetings aren't just about numbers; they're about guiding people through what the market is doing and helping them make sense of it, especially during periods of volatility.

What's interesting is that the stronger the market performs, the more comfortable people become, taking additional risks. It's almost subtle as you don't always notice it happening. Confidence builds, and before long, the level of risk starts to creep higher than what was originally intended.

Over time, this can create a disconnect. The true purpose of taking on risk—the extra return you expect in exchange for that uncertainty can get overlooked. And when that happens, clients may unknowingly expose themselves to more vulnerability than they're prepared for.

My role, as I see it, is to help keep that balance in check, to make sure decisions are grounded not in recent performance, but in what truly aligns with their long-term goals and comfort level.

"Don't look for the needle in the haystack. Just buy the haystack!"

—John Bogle

CHAPTER 11

Distribution of Retirement Plans

Over the years, many of us have benefited from company-sponsored retirement plans, such as 401(k)s, pension plans, and other tax-advantaged savings vehicles designed to support long-term planning. When retirement arrives, and an employee separates from service, one of the key decisions they must make is how to begin taking distributions from the plan.

There are several options available, each with its own implications for taxes, investment flexibility, and future income. One possibility is to leave the money in the employer's plan, if permitted, allowing the assets to continue growing tax-deferred while delaying withdrawals. Alternatively, retirees may choose to roll the funds into an individual retirement account (IRA) to gain greater control over investment options and maintain tax-deferred growth.

Some retirees may opt to take a lump-sum distribution, providing immediate access to their savings. While this can be appealing, it often carries significant tax consequences and, in some cases, early withdrawal penalties. Others may prefer to begin systematic withdrawals from the plan, receiving a steady stream of income on a monthly or quarterly basis. Certain plans, particularly pensions, also offer the option of converting the balance into an annuity to secure guaranteed lifetime income.

The decisions surrounding retirement plan distributions are deeply personal and should be guided by an individual's financial needs, risk tolerance, and long-term goals. Careful planning at this stage can help ensure a smooth transition into retirement and provide a foundation for financial security in the years ahead.

By law, once an individual reaches age 73, they must begin withdrawing a minimum amount from their tax-deferred retirement accounts, such as traditional IRAs, 401(k)s, and certain other employer-sponsored plans. The purpose of RMDs is to ensure that individuals eventually pay taxes on funds that have grown tax-deferred over the years. Failing to take an RMD or withdrawing less than the required amount can result in severe penalties, including a 50% excise tax on the shortfall.

The calculation of an RMD is based on two key factors: the account balance as of December 31 of the previous year and the life expectancy factor provided by IRS tables. The standard formula is straightforward: The account balance is divided by the life expectancy factor to determine the minimum amount that must be withdrawn for the year. For example, if an individual has a retirement account balance of $500,000 at the end of the previous year and the IRS life expectancy factor at their age is 27.4, the RMD for the year would be calculated as $500,000 ÷ 27.4, resulting in approximately $18,248.[39]

Life expectancy factors are published by the IRS in tables that account for the individual's age and, in some cases, the ages of beneficiaries if account ownership is being transferred. These tables are updated periodically to reflect changes in longevity and demographic trends. For married individuals whose spouse is more than 10 years younger and is the sole beneficiary, a special joint life expectancy table is used, which generally reduces the RMD, allowing funds to remain in the account longer and continue growing tax-deferred.

Retirees need to plan their withdrawals carefully. RMDs are taxed

39 IRS Publication 590-B, Distributions from Individual Retirement Arrangements (IRAs).

as ordinary income, and large distributions can impact other aspects of retirement finances, such as Social Security taxation or Medicare premiums. Proper planning may involve spreading distributions over several accounts, timing withdrawals to manage tax brackets, or using strategies such as charitable donations to satisfy RMD requirements without incurring significant tax burdens. We will talk about this in future chapters.

Disclosure:

These results are for illustrative purposes only and should not be deemed a representation of future results. Circumstances, solutions, and/or results are based on specific facts tied to unique client situations. Favorable results cannot be guaranteed even in a similar scenario. Each specific set of circumstances will differ depending on client need and profile. Actual results may be more or may be less than those shown. Past performance does not guarantee future results.

One important planning strategy to consider is converting existing qualified retirement accounts into a Roth IRA. Understanding how this conversion works is crucial, as it can provide long-term benefits not only as a retirement savings tool but also as a valuable component of estate planning.

A Roth IRA is an individual retirement account that allows contributions using after-tax dollars, meaning the funds grow tax-free, and qualified withdrawals in retirement are also tax-free. Unlike traditional IRAs, contributions to a Roth IRA are not tax-deductible, but there are no required minimum distributions (RMDs) during the account holder's lifetime, providing flexibility for retirement planning and potential estate transfer. Contributions are subject to annual limits and income eligibility requirements set by the IRS.

A Roth conversion involves transferring funds from a traditional IRA or other qualified retirement account into a Roth IRA. The amount converted is subject to ordinary income tax in the year of the conversion.

Once in the Roth IRA, any growth in the funds will grow tax-free, and qualified withdrawals in retirement are also tax-free.

A common case study involves an individual who, while still employed, has accumulated substantial savings in a qualified retirement account. Eventually, IRS rules will require them to begin taking minimum distributions. If the conversion does not push this person into a higher tax bracket, portions of the account can be converted to a Roth IRA at the current tax rate, allowing future growth and withdrawals to be tax-free.

In this way, two key components of retirement planning are achieved. First, the existing retirement account will slow its growth due to the distributions, resulting in a smaller RMD amount. At the same time, the newly created Roth IRA can continue to grow tax-free, without any required minimum distributions at any age.

An additional advantage of Roth conversion involves estate planning. Typically, IRA and other retirement account beneficiaries are required to pay taxes on distributions, with one key exception: spouses. When a spouse is designated as the beneficiary, retirement accounts, including 401(k)s, traditional IRAs, and Roth IRAs, can transfer to them tax-free upon the account owner's death. In estate planning terminology, spouses are considered Class A beneficiaries.

Conversion to Roth IRAs adds a key tax savings component, especially for children or beneficiaries other than spouses. You may wonder what happens if the beneficiary of your traditional IRA or 401(k) is a child or someone other than your spouse. In this case, the beneficiary is subject to the 10-Year Rule, which requires the account to be fully distributed within 10 years and can result in significant tax implications.

The 10-year rule is an important consideration for beneficiaries of inherited retirement accounts. Under this rule, which was established by the SECURE Act of 2019, non-spouse beneficiaries of traditional

IRAs and 401(k)s are required to fully withdraw the account balance within 10 years of the original account owner's death.[40]

Unlike traditional required minimum distributions (RMDs), there is no requirement to take annual withdrawals during this period; the account simply must be fully distributed by the end of the 10th year. While this rule accelerates the pace of taxable distributions, beneficiaries have the flexibility to manage withdrawals strategically over the 10 years to minimize their overall tax burden. Spouses and certain other eligible designated beneficiaries, however, can generally continue using lifetime RMDs, preserving tax-deferred growth.

Roth IRAs, on the other hand, provide unique advantages in this context. Because Roth IRAs grow tax-free and qualified withdrawals are not subject to income taxes, beneficiaries are not burdened by the tax implications that apply to traditional accounts. Furthermore, if a child or other non-spouse is designated as the beneficiary of a Roth IRA, the account proceeds are generally not subject to the 10-year rule, allowing greater flexibility in timing withdrawals while preserving the tax-free growth of the account. This makes Roth IRAs a powerful tool for intergenerational wealth transfer, offering both income tax advantages and more control over distributions for heirs.

It is essential to regularly review beneficiary designations to ensure they are accurate and reflect your current intentions. The worst-case scenario occurs when no beneficiary is listed. In that case, the retirement account may be subject to probate, and the funds could be taxed both as a distribution and as part of the estate, under the rules for income in respect of a decedent.

Retirement account distributions can affect both Social Security benefits and Medicare costs. Withdrawals from traditional IRAs, 401(k)s, or other tax-deferred accounts are counted as taxable income,

---

40 SECURE Act of 2019, Public Law 116-94.

which can increase the portion of Social Security benefits subject to taxation.

Additionally, higher income levels may raise Medicare Part B and Part D premiums under the Income-Related Monthly Adjustment Amount (IRMAA) rules.[41] Careful planning of distributions, such as timing withdrawals or using Roth conversions, can help manage taxable income, reduce taxes on Social Security benefits, and limit Medicare premium increases.

As I mentioned previously, Roth IRA withdrawals are not subject to income tax and will not affect Social Security or (IRMAA) rules.

I remember sitting down with Mark not too long ago. He had just received news that many people would consider a blessing—a significant inheritance that instantly changed his financial picture.

But before we even got into the details of the inheritance, I wanted to take a step back and understand his full situation. As we talked, Mark shared that he already had about $1.4 million in his IRA. He wasn't married, had no children, and was living comfortably on a $75,000 pension along with about $37,000 a year from Social Security.

On the surface, everything looked solid. But as we dug a little deeper, I could see a potential issue developing down the road.

I explained to Mark that his IRA, while a great asset, could eventually become a tax problem. Once he's required to take required minimum distributions, those withdrawals could push his income significantly higher. That, in turn, could trigger increased Medicare premiums and cause more of his Social Security to become taxable under IRMAA rules.

It's one of those situations where success quietly creates its own set of challenges.

So, we started talking about being proactive. I suggested that we consider converting a portion or even all of his traditional IRA into a

41 Social Security Administration: Medicare Premiums: Rules for higher income beneficiaries (IRMAA).

Roth IRA over time. By doing this strategically, we could potentially reduce or eliminate future RMDs, better control his taxable income, and limit his exposure to those additional Medicare-related costs.

But what really resonated with Mark was the bigger picture.

This wasn't just about taxes today; it was about control, flexibility, and creating a more efficient plan. And while he doesn't have children, Roth also gives him a powerful estate planning tool, allowing whatever remains to pass on in a far more tax-efficient way, without the burden of heavy taxable withdrawals over a compressed 10-year period.

By the end of the conversation, the inheritance wasn't just a windfall; it became an opportunity. An opportunity to reshape his plan, reduce future risk, and put him in a stronger, more predictable position for the years ahead.

"A retired husband is often a wife's full-time job."

—Ella Harris

CHAPTER 12

The Windfall Phenomenon

As outlined in the chart in Chapter 1, the Silent Generation, those born between 1928 and 1945, now range in age from about 80 to 98 years old. Throughout their lifetimes, this generation has witnessed an extraordinary moment in history and adapted to countless social and financial changes. Consider the contrast between past and present: Many members of this generation grew up during the early years of automobile development, yet they now live in an era where self-driving cars are becoming a reality.

After World War II, immigration became a crucial force driving the growth of the United States. European immigrants, arriving from a war-torn continent, came to America in search of a new beginning and the promise of a land filled with opportunity. Most arrived with little or no money, armed only with determination, hard work, and an unwavering refusal to accept failure as their fate.

My father was born in 1933, into a world that demanded toughness before a child even had a chance to grow up. He didn't fight in the war himself because he was too young, but the war shaped everything around him. His father, my grandfather, had served, and back home in Sicily, life was anything but easy.

He was one of twelve children, raised in a small town that was heavily bombed during the war. There was no real sense of safety, just survival. Food was scarce, shelter was uncertain, and healthcare was almost nonexistent. He often spoke of those years not with bitterness, but with a quiet understanding of what it meant to go without. Those experiences didn't break him; they built something inside of him. A resilience. A determination that would stay with him for the rest of his life.

In 1958, at 28 years old, he came to America with very little, but with a mindset shaped by hardship and persistence. He worked tirelessly, saved what he could, and approached money with a level of discipline that only comes from knowing what it's like to have none.

By the time he turned 40, he had already achieved something remarkable. He owned two homes. One was where he raised his family, and the other he rented out, creating an additional stream of income. For many, that would have been enough. A sign that they had "made it."

But my father wasn't wired that way.

At 42, he decided that most people would have been too afraid to take. He sold both homes, took on significant debt, and bet everything on a bakery.

It wasn't just any bakery; it became *the* bakery. Over time, it grew into the largest wholesale bakery in Bergen County, New Jersey, supplying restaurants, schools, hospitals, and grocery stores across the state. It was a 24-hour operation that never closed, and neither, it seemed, did he.

He worked relentlessly. Long hours, constant pressure, but he never complained. To him, this wasn't a sacrifice. It was an opportunity.

Everything he built came from that same place: determination, resilience, and an unwillingness to accept anything less than forward progress. His success wasn't luck. It was earned, day by day, through grit and belief in something better. He was part of the Silent Generation.

Many people who have parents or grandparents who immigrated to this country can share stories that are both similar and unique in their own ways. One common thread among them is that, through hard work and perseverance, they managed to build financial stability and often to amass a modest fortune over the course of their lifetimes.

The reason I share these stories is to highlight the habits that this generation developed over the years. Their life experiences taught them the value of saving and hard work, which eventually led many to become small business owners. Over time, their perseverance and discipline allowed them to build and maintain a significant amount of wealth.

My father passed away at the age of 83, leaving behind a substantial inheritance for my mother, who is now 92. The amount of wealth he left her far exceeds what she could ever need or spend in her remaining years.

After many years of thoughtful planning and the establishment of a will and trust, the orderly succession and distribution of her estate will take place upon her passing.

This Silent Generation is expected to transfer an unprecedented amount of wealth to their heirs in the coming years, estimated at over $18 trillion in the United States alone.[42] Some estimates have this number much higher.

Globally, members are expected to pass down an estimated $30 trillion to $40 trillion in assets to younger generations over the next 20 years, marking one of the largest intergenerational transfers of wealth in history.[43]

It is important to recognize that the next generation poised to inherit this wealth may be more inclined to spend it imprudently, often on extravagant and unnecessary lifestyles.

In my own experience, I've seen how something meant to be a lasting gift, an inheritance built over generations, can slowly be worn away by spending that wasn't truly necessary or thought through.

What's been even harder to witness at times is how these situations can affect families. I've seen moments where, instead of bringing

42 *U.S. High-Net-Worth and Ultra-High-Net-Worth Markets 2023: The Great Wealth Transfer*, Boston, MA. Cerulli Associates, 2023.

43 *Billionaires Insights 2022: The Great Wealth Transfer*, UBS Group AG and PwC, Zurich, 2022.

people together, an estate creates tension and misunderstanding. Relationships that once felt strong can become strained, and in some cases, disagreements over assets lead to divisions that are difficult to repair.

It's a reminder to me that wealth is never just about money; it's about the people it touches, and the importance of planning with both care and intention.

If you are facing this situation or are a part of it somehow, it is important to remain actively engaged with both siblings and parents to preserve the legacy of their hard work and to resolve any disputes with fairness and reason. I take great pride in my family's accomplishments and feel a deep sense of loyalty to my siblings and, above all, to my mother and father. For me, family has always been, and continues to be, the most important and enduring foundation in life.

Unfortunately, for many families, this is not the case. A significant portion of the inheritances I've mentioned is often consumed by litigation over estate disputes. Allowing a judge to determine how one's hard-earned estate is divided can be disheartening and contrary to the intentions of those who sacrificed and worked diligently to build it.

The generational windfall now underway is a once-in-a-lifetime phenomenon, expected to unfold over the next 12 to 15 years. Economists estimate that members of the Silent Generation and early baby boomers will transfer more wealth in the United States than any other nation, with global estimates ranging between $100 and $120 trillion. [44] This massive transfer of assets, spanning real estate, investments, and family businesses, represents the largest redistribution of private wealth in modern history.

"Family is not an important thing; it's everything."

—Michael J. Fox

44 *Billionaires Insights 2022: The Great Wealth Transfer*, UBS Group AG and PwC, Zurich, 2022.

CHAPTER 13

The "Sandwich Generation"

The term Sandwich Generation refers to a group of adults typically in their mid-30s to 50s who find themselves simultaneously caring for their aging parents while still supporting their own children. This dual responsibility places them "sandwiched" between two generations that depend on them for financial, emotional, and sometimes physical support. As life expectancy has increased and children remain financially dependent for longer periods, the pressures on this group have intensified significantly in recent decades.[45]

Members of the Sandwich Generation often struggle to balance competing demands on their time and resources. Many face the emotional burden of watching their parents' health decline while also trying to nurture children, advance their careers, and save for retirement.

Financially, they may contribute to their parents' medical or living expenses while covering college tuition or housing costs for their children. According to a 2023 Pew Research Center report, nearly one in five adults in the United States now fits the description of being part of the Sandwich Generation, with middle-aged women slightly more likely to assume the role of caregiver.[46]

---

45 Dorothy A. Miller, *The 'Sandwich' Generation: Adult Children of the Aging.*

46 Kim Parker and Rachel Minkin, *About One-in-Five U.S. Adults Are in the Sandwich Generation.*

The implications of this growing demographic trend are far-reaching. From a social perspective, the strain can lead to increased stress, burnout, and challenges to mental health. Economically, many in the Sandwich Generation find themselves depleting their savings, delaying retirement, or accumulating debt to meet the needs of both generations. This generation faces unique financial and emotional strain because they're caught between supporting parents living longer than past generations and adult children taking longer to reach financial independence.[47] In many cases, workplace flexibility, family-friendly policies, and social support systems play a crucial role in helping this generation manage these overlapping responsibilities.

Understanding the challenges faced by the Sandwich Generation highlights the need for broader societal and policy support. Expanding affordable elder care options, promoting financial literacy, and encouraging multigenerational planning can help alleviate the pressures this generation faces. Without meaningful interventions, the growing demands on these individuals could have long-term consequences for families, employers, and the broader economy. Let's investigate some planning strategies that can help alleviate the pressures.

As discussed in earlier chapters, it is essential that all children of elderly parents, or any involved family members, take an active role in both decision-making and caregiving. Open communication and a unified approach are critical so that everyone shares the same understanding, expectations, and goals. While most individuals act with sincere and well-meaning intentions, those efforts can sometimes be misunderstood or perceived as self-interest. As the saying goes, "*The road to hell is paved with good intentions,*" a reminder that even good motives must be paired with clarity, transparency, and alignment.

---

47 Amy M. Loree, *The Financial and Emotional Burden of the Sandwich Generation,* Journal of Family and Economic Issues.

A comprehensive list of all assets, including an inventory of real property, should be compiled and professionally appraised. This process helps identify the total value of the estate and reveal any potential shortfall in available cash to meet immediate needs or expenses. The inventory should include bank accounts, investment portfolios, personal property such as automobiles, jewelry, artwork, heirlooms, and collectibles, as well as insurance policies. Liabilities, including mortgages, credit card balances, and unpaid taxes, should also be clearly listed. Once the full inventory is completed, it should be shared with all interested family members or other relevant parties. Any uncertainties or omissions should be discussed openly, and all participants should acknowledge and sign off on the finalized documentation to ensure transparency and mutual understanding.

I recently had a phone conversation with a woman who opened up about how helpless she had been feeling. It was a heartfelt and emotional discussion, shaped by the challenges of family dynamics and the weight of financial responsibility. She shared that her sister had taken the lead in managing their mother's finances, and over time, largely due to a lack of open communication, the assets were ultimately depleted.

It was clear that her sister's intentions came from a place of care, but by making decisions on her own rather than involving her, it created confusion and concern. Without going into specifics, the absence of communication took a lasting toll, not only financially, but emotionally. In the end, what remained was a sense of hurt, lingering resentment, and a relationship that had been deeply strained, despite both wanting what was best for their mother.

The next step is to evaluate the cost of additional care services, whether that involves hiring an in-home aide or a private caregiver to assist with day-to-day needs. Once an approximate cost has been established, the available assets can be evaluated to determine how funds should be allocated to cover necessary expenses.

As you navigate through this process, nothing will be based on consistency. Every day will be fraught with new challenges. Aging individuals, especially those in need of care, eventually worsen as time goes on. Dementia, Alzheimer's, or physical impairments rarely move in a positive direction, and the focus should be on daily care and comfort.

"Life is a seesaw, and I am standing dead center, still and balanced: living with kids on one side, living with parents on the other."

—Catherine Newman

CHAPTER 14

Leaving a Legacy

Leaving a legacy means shaping what remains of you after your lifetime, through the values you pass on, the relationships you build, and the impact you make on others. It is not limited to money or possessions, but rather reflects how you lived, what you stood for, and how you influenced the lives around you.

A legacy is created through everyday actions. The way you treat family, friends, and strangers often leaves the deepest impression. Kindness, integrity, responsibility, and perseverance are traits that endure when they are modeled consistently. People may forget specific words or events, but they remember how someone made them feel and the example that was set.

Legacy also involves preparation and intention. Planning for your future, which is a journey, not a task, requires an ongoing self-assessment and a personal inventory of your achievements. Guiding children, mentoring others, or organizing personal and financial affairs demonstrates care for those who will carry on after you.

Clear direction reduces confusion, protects loved ones, and reflects thoughtfulness beyond one's own lifetime.

Leaving a legacy is about meaning rather than memory alone. It is the quiet assurance that your life contributed something of value, that others are better because you were part of their journey. A true legacy lives on in character, influence, and the positive difference made in the world.

Part of leaving a legacy requires you to be selfless, not in death but in life. One's legacy doesn't begin at death but is an ongoing story through the roads of life. Many selfless acts can be described as actions for the benefit of others, without expecting recognition, reward, or personal gain. It derives from a place of compassion and understanding that helping others strengthens relationships and communities.

Many of you may find fulfillment in serving through volunteer work, participating on local boards, or even pursuing public office. This stage of life may be an ideal time to do so, especially as you transition into empty nesters. With parenting responsibilities reduced, these opportunities allow you to give back to your community without taking time away from raising a family.

I've been fortunate to spend many years in the financial services industry, helping clients understand the value of building, protecting, and ultimately enjoying the wealth they've worked so hard for. Along the way, I wrote a book that became a number one bestseller on Amazon, something I'm deeply grateful for, and I'm currently working on two more. Writing has become a meaningful part of how I hope to leave a lasting impact: by sharing what I've learned, helping others feel more confident in their financial decisions, and encouraging them to pursue their own version of financial independence.

My son, who serves in law enforcement, has a bright path ahead of him once he completes his career in public safety. With his master's degree in the field, he'll have the flexibility to explore opportunities in education, perhaps as a teacher or a resource officer in a local school. I could also see him continuing to give back through public service organizations, using his experience to mentor and support young people as they find their way.

My spouse's father was an engineer with Caterpillar, but what truly defined him was how he gave his time to others. Before he passed, he dedicated countless hours volunteering with Habitat for Humanity, helping build and improve homes for families in need. He's remembered not just for his career, but for his kindness, the quiet, consistent way he chose to make a difference in the lives of others.

As these examples show, there are so many meaningful ways to give back, often right within our own communities. There are always organizations looking for people who are simply willing to show up and share their time, their skills, or even just their presence. Whether it's through groups like Rotary, UNICO, faith-based communities, veterans' organizations, or local senior centers, the opportunities to make a difference are truly all around us.

In the end, creating a legacy and sharing your gifts isn't about recognition or accolades. It's much more personal than that. It's about finding a sense of purpose that feels genuine and lasting. Rather than focusing only on milestones or achievements, it's about building a way of life, one rooted in giving, connection, and meaning, that quietly adds value not only to your own life, but to the lives of others as well.

Creating your legacy and sharing your talents is not about recognition, trophies, or awards. It is about discovering and sustaining a sense of purpose. Rather than focusing solely on achievements or end goals, it is about building a meaningful system, a way of living that consistently brings value to your life and to others.

In retirement, this often requires repurposing yourself. The structure once provided by a career must be replaced with intentional activities that foster fulfillment, connection, and contribution. The system you create should allow you to end each day with a positive and healthy sense of accomplishment, knowing your time was spent with intention and meaning.

Acts of service, mentorship, and generosity provide this foundation. They reinforce self-worth, encourage personal growth, and strengthen community bonds. While recognition may never come, it is unnecessary. No genuine good deed goes unnoticed but leaves an imprint on others and quietly becomes part of a legacy defined by purpose, impact, and lasting influence.

"Part of leaving your legacy is not worrying what everyone is saying about it."

— Fabolous

CHAPTER 15

Wills, Trusts, Foundations, and Charitable Giving

Wills, trusts, foundations, and charitable giving can range from very simple arrangements to highly complex structures, depending on personal circumstances and goals. While the details may vary, these tools are essential components of responsible planning for most individuals and couples.

At their core, they provide clarity, protection, and direction. A well-crafted will or trust helps ensure that assets are distributed according to one's wishes, reduces the potential for confusion or conflict, and can ease the emotional burden placed on loved ones. Charitable strategies and foundations, whether modest or expansive, allow individuals to align their values with their resources and extend their impact beyond their lifetime.

Regardless of size or complexity, the importance lies in having a plan in place. Thoughtful preparation brings peace of mind, safeguards what has been built, and reflects care for both family and the community. In every case, these planning tools are not optional but a necessary step in creating order, purpose, and a legacy.

Let's take each component of this chapter and break it down into a simple explanation.

A will is a legal document created by an individual that clearly states their final wishes upon death. It outlines how assets are to be distributed, who will be responsible for carrying out those wishes, and, when applicable, who will serve as guardian for minor children.

Beyond directing the transfer of property, a will provides clarity and structure during a time of emotional difficulty. It helps prevent misunderstandings, reduces the likelihood of disputes among heirs, and ensures that personal intentions are honored. Without a will, state laws determine how assets are divided, which may not align with an individual's preferences.

A properly drafted will is a foundational element of estate planning. It reflects responsibility, foresight, and care for loved ones, offering both guidance and peace of mind by ensuring one's legacy is handled according to their intentions.

Everyone who has accumulated property during their lifetime has created an estate. An estate includes real estate, bank accounts, investments, and personal belongings, ranging from valuable assets like a home or stocks to everyday items such as a watch or a bicycle. Upon death, these assets must be properly managed and distributed to heirs according to the individual's wishes, typically through a will, trust, or other estate planning tools.

On a more personal note, I've seen firsthand how important it is for families to have even the most basic plans in place. In our role as fiduciaries, one of the conversations we come back to time and time again is the importance of having a will. It's not always an easy topic. Some clients feel uncomfortable; others simply aren't ready, but it's one we approach with care and patience.

There have been times when, despite thoughtful conversations, a client decides not to move forward. In those moments, we gently take an extra step. We ask them to sign a simple acknowledgment, not as a formality, but to make sure they fully understand our recommendation and the potential consequences of leaving things unplanned.

For us, it's never about paperwork. It's about making sure our clients feel informed, respected, and protected. More than anything, it's about helping them take even small, thoughtful steps toward safeguarding the people and legacy they care about most.

The simplest type of will is often called an "I love you" will, typically created between two spouses. This straightforward document directs that all property owned by one spouse be transferred to the other upon death. Each spouse names the other as the executor of their will, ensuring that all assets are passed on directly to the surviving spouse without complication. This type of will is easy to create and provides a clear, uncomplicated way to protect each other's interests.

Probated property refers to assets that are subject to the legal process of probate after an individual's death. Probate is the court-supervised procedure through which a deceased person's estate is validated, debts and taxes are settled, and remaining assets are distributed to heirs or beneficiaries according to a will or state law if no will exists. Probated property typically includes assets that are solely in the decedent's name and do not have designated beneficiaries, such as certain bank accounts, real estate, personal property, and investments.[48] This is why having a will is essential. Few people would want a court to determine how their estate is distributed. A properly drafted will provides clear instructions and helps avoid unnecessary probate, ensuring that assets are passed according to one's wishes rather than default state laws.

Assets with named beneficiaries, such as life insurance policies, retirement accounts, and accounts designated as Transfer on Death (TOD) or Payable on Death (POD), are generally considered non-probate assets. These assets need not be mentioned in the will. These assets operate under separate legal frameworks that prioritize the beneficiary designation over instructions in a will.

---

48 Estate Planning Texts and Guides – such as Nool's Estate Planning Basics and The Complete Guide to Wills and Estates.

The will, a formal legal instrument, is submitted to the appropriate local probate court, accompanied by a certified copy of the decedent's death certificate. This presentation initiates the probate process, which is the judicial procedure for validating a will and overseeing the administration of an estate. Upon receipt, the court clerk, or a designated official, undertakes a preliminary review of these documents. The primary purpose of this initial examination is to ascertain the authenticity of the will and to ensure its proper recording within the court's official archives.

The court can also issue "letters of testamentary," a formal legal document that officially identifies the executor or executrix of an estate. This document grants the named individual the legal authority to manage the deceased person's assets and carry out the instructions outlined in the will. Essentially, it serves as the court's recognition of the executor's role and powers in administering the estate.

As the decedent's accounts are registered, a tax identification number (TIN) will be required. An accountant or CPA can obtain this number directly from the IRS. This TIN is then used to prepare and file the decedent's final tax return, ensuring all taxes are accurately reported and settled.

Much of this process requires the guidance of both an attorney and a tax professional. Attempting to navigate these matters alone is not recommended, as professional expertise is essential to ensure everything is handled correctly. The context of this discussion to this point is to give you a basic understanding of the importance of having a will.

I would like to shift our discussion to trusts, which are essential tools in estate planning. Broadly speaking, there are two primary types: revocable trusts and irrevocable trusts. A trust typically involves two main parties: the grantor and the beneficiary. The grantor is the individual who transfers property or assets into the trust, thereby creating the trust corpus. The beneficiary is the person or entity entitled to receive benefits or distributions from the trust in accordance with its terms.

In addition, a trust requires a trustee, who is responsible for managing the trust assets and administering the trust as directed. In a revocable trust, the grantor often serves as the trustee and may appoint a co-trustee as well as a successor trustee to step in if needed. In the case of an irrevocable trust, however, the grantor must appoint an independent, disinterested party to serve as trustee, as the grantor relinquishes control over the trust assets.

A trust may be established either during the grantor's lifetime or upon the grantor's death through the provisions of a will. When a trust is created at death, it is referred to as a testamentary trust. Trusts are designed to serve specific and clearly defined purposes. For example, a trust may be used to hold and manage assets for children who have not yet reached legal adulthood, or it may be structured to provide ongoing care, support, and financial management for beneficiaries over time. While young children are a common example, trust may be established for the benefit of any individual or entity.

The reason the concept of a testamentary trust is important is that, during a person's lifetime, there may not be sufficient assets available to fund a trust. In such cases, a life insurance policy is often used. Upon death, the proceeds from the policy can be directed into the trust, thereby funding it at that time. The trustee, acting as a fiduciary, is legally obligated to manage the trust assets in accordance with the terms of the trust and applicable laws.

Many types of trust documents may be used to shelter and protect an individual's assets during their lifetime and after their passing. However, it is important to remember that trust is a separate legal entity and carries ongoing responsibilities. As such, a trust typically requires annual tax filings and the reporting of any income generated by the assets held within it.

A few examples of trust documents are a special needs trust. This trust is set up for a disabled child or person who will need ongoing care after the primary caretaker passes.

A Qualified Personal Residential Trust, QRPT, allows a person to place the primary residence into an irrevocable trust, while retaining the right to live in the home for the owner's lifetime or a specified number of years, at which point it will pass to the named beneficiaries.

An Irrevocable Life Insurance Trust, ILIT, allows a person to place a life insurance policy into an irrevocable trust. This is a tool designed to remove life insurance proceeds from the taxable estate of a decedent.

A QTIP trust, short for Qualified Terminable Interest Property trust, is a type of estate-planning trust most used by married couples to provide for a surviving spouse while ultimately controlling where the assets go after that spouse's death. When the first spouse passes, assets are placed into the QTIP trust for the benefit of the surviving spouse. The surviving spouse will receive all income generated by the trust for his or her lifetime, typically paid annually. However, the spouse does not have control over the corpus of the trust. After the surviving spouse passes, the corpus of the trust will be distributed to the final beneficiary, who can be either a person or a charity.

This brings us to our next discussion on charitable giving and the use of creating a foundation. Foundations and charitable trusts are established primarily to carry out an individual's philanthropic goals and charitable giving intentions. To receive favorable tax treatment, the trust or foundation must comply with specific guidelines established by the IRS. It is strongly recommended that individuals work closely with a qualified CPA or tax professional when considering or establishing this type of charitable structure.

A foundation is established as a legal entity and may be funded either during an individual's lifetime or at death. Establishing a foundation during one's lifetime offers several advantages, including the ability to actively participate in philanthropic efforts and decision-making. It may also provide immediate tax benefits, help create a lasting charitable legacy for the individual and their family, and offer greater control over charitable giving compared to making outright donations. Foundations are complex entities that require the guidance of legal counsel, and they are typically established by individuals with significant financial resources.

Charitable giving, on the other hand, has become increasingly common and is an approach many individuals are now choosing to pursue. Many insurance and investment companies offer IRS-approved products that require only the designation of a chosen charitable beneficiary. The basic requirement is that the charity be a verifiable 501(c)(3) organization. This ensures the charity has a tax-exempt designation by the IRS as to its non-profit organization status and operates exclusively for religious, educational, medical, or scientific purposes. Many insurance and investment companies offer IRS-approved products that require only the designation of a chosen charitable beneficiary.

Approved charitable trusts are known as Charitable Remainder Trusts (CRTs). The two most used types are the Charitable Remainder Unitrust (CRUT) and the Charitable Remainder Annuity Trust (CRAT).

The Charitable Remainder Unitrust is a trust in which a corpus or property is made into the trust. This amount is immediately available as a charitable income tax deduction. The income of the trust is paid annually to the beneficiary for life. Because the value fluctuates based on the income generated, it may increase over time. This trust is best suited for individuals seeking income growth potential. Additional contributions can be made.

The Charitable Remainder Annuity Trust is similar, but for two major differences: the value of the income does not change, and it is fixed. In addition, no future contributions may be made after the initial deposit. This is best suited for individuals seeking a predictable, steady income.

These are strategies I've had the opportunity to use many times over the years, but one experience in particular has always stayed with me.

I remember working with an elderly client who had built a meaningful portfolio of highly appreciated stock. The dividends provided her with a comfortable stream of income, something she depended on and appreciated. She didn't have any close family, and her will named two distant relatives she hadn't spoken to in years. As we talked, it became clear that while she had done well financially, her plan didn't truly reflect what mattered most to her at this stage of her life.

We spent time exploring her options and eventually introduced the idea of Charitable Remainder Unitrust. It wasn't a quick decision; it was a thoughtful process. In the end, she found comfort in knowing she could continue receiving the income she relied on, while also reducing the burden of taxes on her estate. Just as important, she was able to leave something meaningful to a cause she genuinely cared about.

What stood out most wasn't the strategy itself, but the sense of peace she felt once everything was aligned with her values. It was a reminder that good planning isn't just about numbers, it's about helping people feel confident that their legacy reflects who they are and what they believe in.

Another situation that comes to mind involved a client who had owned a life insurance policy for many years. As we sat together reviewing his overall plan, he began to reflect not just on his assets but also on what he truly wanted them to accomplish for his family and beyond.

Over time, we worked through a thoughtful strategy together. He chose to place the policy into an Irrevocable Life Insurance Trust, and from there, name a Charitable Remainder Annuity Trust as the beneficiary. His hope was simple and heartfelt; he wanted to make sure his two children were cared for throughout their lives, while also leaving something meaningful behind for a cause close to his heart.

When the time came, the life insurance proceeds would fund the trust, providing his children with a steady, reliable income each year for the rest of their lives. And after they were gone, whatever remained would pass on to St. Jude Children's Research Hospital, a place he deeply believed in.

What made this plan so special wasn't just how it worked, but why it was created. It allowed him to take care of his family in a very real way, while also extending his generosity far beyond his lifetime. It reflected both his love for his children and his desire to make a lasting difference in the world.

This approach highlights the importance of integrating life insurance, trust planning, and charitable giving to help achieve financial, familial, and philanthropic goals in a coordinated and tax-efficient manner.

Charitable giving is something I gently encourage all my clients to think about in whatever way they feel is meaningful to them. It's also important to me personally. Each year, our firm supports several local charities, and it's a responsibility I don't take lightly.

For me, it's never really been about the tax benefits. It's about the privilege of being able to give back, to play even a small role in helping those who may be going through difficult times. There's a quiet sense of fulfillment that comes from knowing that, in some way, you've made a positive difference in someone else's life. Here is a list of Charitable Organizations we give to:

- St Judes Children's Hospital
- Hackensack Meridian Health Foundation
- Local Boy Scouts
- Paramus Community Pantry
- Trinity Church
- SOROPTIMIST
- United States Navy Memorial

The charitable entities and/or fundraising opportunities described herein are note endorsed by or affiliated with Cetera Investment Services LLC or its affiliates. Our philanthropic interests are personal to us and are not reviewed, sponsored or approved by Cetera.

"We can't help everyone, but everyone can help someone."
—Ronald Reagan

CHAPTER 16

The Time to Act Is Now

Throughout this book, we have explored many aspects of retirement and financial planning. We have discussed demographics, healthcare, Social Security, housing, asset allocation, retirement distributions, estate planning, charitable giving, and the importance of leaving a meaningful legacy. Each chapter has focused on a different part of the journey, yet they all share one common theme: planning matters.

Retirement is not a single event that occurs on the day you stop working. It is a long and evolving phase of life that requires preparation, adaptability, and thoughtful decision-making. The financial choices made today will determine not only the comfort of your retirement years but also the security and well-being of those who depend on you.

One of the most important lessons to take from this book is that the time to act is now.

Too many people delay financial planning. They assume there will always be time later to organize their finances, write a will, evaluate their investments, or develop a retirement income strategy. Unfortunately, life rarely operates on a convenient schedule. Unexpected events such as illness, market volatility, job loss, or family emergencies can quickly change circumstances. Planning is not about predicting the future perfectly. It is about preparing for uncertainty so that you and your family can face whatever comes with confidence and stability.

For much of our working lives, we focus on accumulation. We save, invest, and build assets with the expectation that one day those resources will provide financial independence. When retirement finally arrives, the focus shifts from accumulation to distribution and preservation. This transition can be challenging because the strategies that helped build wealth are not always the same strategies needed to sustain it. In retirement, individuals must consider how long their money needs to last, how to manage taxes, how to manage healthcare costs, and how to protect their assets against inflation and market fluctuations.

At the same time, retirement offers something far more valuable than financial freedom alone: time. Time to pursue passions. Time to spend with family. Time to contribute to the community. Time to reflect on the life you have built. The financial planning decisions you make today will determine how freely you can enjoy that time.

THE REALITY OF LONGEVITY

One of the defining characteristics of the baby boomer generation is longevity. Advances in medicine, nutrition, and healthcare have extended life expectancy far beyond what previous generations experienced. Many retirees today will live twenty-five to thirty years or longer after leaving the workforce. While this is certainly a blessing, it also presents financial challenges. A retirement that lasts three decades requires careful planning to ensure that income remains stable and assets continue to grow enough to keep pace with inflation.

Healthcare costs, long-term care needs, and changing tax laws can significantly impact retirement finances. Without proper preparation, even individuals who have accumulated substantial savings during their working years may find themselves facing financial uncertainty later in life.

The key is to build a strategy that balances growth, income, and risk management. This requires understanding how different financial tools, such as Social Security benefits, retirement accounts, annuities, and investment portfolios work together to support long-term financial security.

Throughout this book, we have discussed the importance of organizing your financial life. This begins with clarity. Knowing what you own, what you owe, and how your assets are structured is the first step toward effective planning. Every household should maintain a clear inventory of its financial life. This includes bank accounts, investment portfolios, retirement plans, insurance policies, real estate holdings, and personal property. Equally important is documenting liabilities such as mortgages, credit obligations, and tax responsibilities.

This information should not exist only in one person's memory. It should be organized and accessible to trusted family members or advisors who may need to assist in managing these affairs if circumstances change. Transparency within families helps avoid confusion and prevents many of the conflicts that can arise during difficult times.

Building wealth is only part of the financial journey. Protecting that wealth is equally important. A properly structured estate plan ensures that your assets are distributed according to your wishes and that your loved ones are not burdened with unnecessary legal complications. At a minimum, every individual should have a will in place. A will provides clear instructions regarding how property should be distributed and identifies the person responsible for conducting those instructions.

Trusts may also play an important role in estate planning. Depending on personal circumstances, trusts can provide tax advantages, protect assets, and help manage distributions for beneficiaries over time. Estate planning is not only about transferring wealth. It is about providing clarity and protection for the people who matter most to you. Without a plan, the courts will ultimately determine how assets are distributed according to state law. Few individuals would choose to leave such important decisions in the hands of strangers.

Financial planning is not only a technical exercise involving investments and legal documents. It is also a family matter. Many of the challenges discussed throughout this book involve multiple generations. The Sandwich Generation, for example, often finds itself responsible for caring for aging parents while simultaneously supporting children. Open communication between family members is essential in these situations. Discussing financial expectations, caregiving responsibilities, and long-term planning strategies can prevent misunderstandings and reduce emotional stress during difficult times.

While these conversations may not always be easy, they are far easier than resolving disputes after problems arise. Families that plan together are far more likely to preserve both their wealth and their relationships.

We are currently witnessing one of the most significant economic transitions in modern history. As members of the Silent Generation and early baby boomers age, trillions of dollars in wealth will be transferred to younger generations. This intergenerational transfer represents both an opportunity and a responsibility. For those who inherit assets, the challenge is learning how to manage and preserve that wealth responsibly. Many individuals who receive large inheritances are unprepared for the financial decisions that accompany them.

For those passing wealth to the next generation, thoughtful planning is essential to ensure that assets are transferred efficiently and according to their wishes. Estate planning, charitable giving strategies, and family communication all play important roles in preserving generational wealth and honoring the efforts of those who built it.

Financial planning ultimately serves the larger purpose of living a meaningful life. As individuals transition into retirement, many discover that the structure provided by a career must be replaced with new forms of purpose and fulfillment. Some choose to continue working at a reduced capacity. Others pursue volunteer opportunities, mentorship roles, or community leadership positions.

Giving back to the community can provide tremendous satisfaction. Organizations such as Rotary, Habitat for Humanity, faith-based groups, veterans' organizations, and local charities rely heavily on the time and talents of volunteers. These contributions may not always receive recognition, but their impact is profound. Acts of service strengthen communities and create a legacy that extends far beyond financial wealth.

Many individuals discover that charitable giving becomes an important part of their legacy planning. For some, this involves simple annual donations to organizations they care about. For others, it may involve more structured strategies such as charitable trusts or private foundations. Charitable planning allows individuals to align their financial resources with their personal values. It also offers potential tax advantages when structured appropriately. However, the true reward of charitable giving is not the tax deduction. It is the knowledge that your efforts have made a positive difference in the lives of others. In many ways, philanthropy represents the highest expression of financial success.

WHY PROFESSIONAL GUIDANCE MATTERS

The financial landscape today is complex. Tax laws change frequently. Investment markets fluctuate. Retirement planning strategies continue to evolve. For most individuals, navigating these issues alone can be overwhelming. This is why professional guidance is so important. A knowledgeable financial advisor can help individuals develop a comprehensive strategy that integrates investment management, tax planning, retirement income planning, and estate planning.

The best advisors do more than simply recommend financial products. They serve as partners in the planning process, helping clients make informed decisions and adjust strategies as circumstances change. Choosing the right advisor requires careful consideration. Look for professionals who function as fiduciaries, meaning they are legally obligated to place their clients' interests ahead of their own. Seek individuals with strong credentials, experience, and a reputation for integrity. Equally important is trust. Financial planning involves deep personal decisions and collaborating with an advisor you respect and feel comfortable with is essential.

Here are two stories to illustrate the difference in financial advisors.

Story One: The Value of Sound Advice

When Robert and Linda walked into my office, they were both recently retired and feeling uneasy about the future. Robert had spent thirty-five years working as a mechanical engineer, while Linda had been a school administrator. Together, they had accumulated what they believed was a comfortable nest egg, which was roughly $1.2 million in retirement accounts, along with their home and modest savings. Despite their disciplined saving, they had one lingering concern about their money lasting.

Robert had always managed the family's investments himself. Over the years, he had built a portfolio largely consisting of individual stocks, many of them companies he admired and had followed for decades. Some had performed extremely well, but the portfolio lacked diversification and produced inconsistent income.

I asked...

"What does retirement look like for you?"

Linda spoke first. "We want to travel while we're still healthy. And we'd like to help our grandchildren with college someday."

Robert added another concern. "My biggest fear is running out of money."

Over the next several meetings, my office carefully reviewed their financial picture. We analyzed their Social Security benefits, evaluated their investments, reviewed their tax situation, and helped them estimate future healthcare expenses. What Robert and Linda discovered surprised them.

Although their portfolio had grown nicely over time, the heavy concentration in a few stocks created significant risks. A market downturn could severely impact their retirement income. In addition, they had no clear withdrawal strategy and had never considered how taxes might affect their retirement distributions.

We proposed a comprehensive plan. First, we gradually diversified their investments into a balanced portfolio aligned with their risk tolerance and retirement timeline. Second, he helped them establish a bucket strategy, placing several years of living expenses in conservative investments while keeping a portion of their assets invested for long-term growth. Third, we recommend delaying Robert's Social Security benefits until age 70, which significantly increased their guaranteed income for life. Finally, we worked with their estate attorney to ensure their will, trust, and beneficiary designations were properly coordinated.

Over the following years, Robert and Linda began to feel confident, something they had not experienced before with their financial situation.

They traveled to Italy, visited national parks across the country, and spent more time with their grandchildren. Their retirement income arrived consistently each month. Robert and Linda reported feeling more comfortable with the financial planning approach after reviewing their strategy.

One afternoon, while sitting on the porch of their lake house, Robert turned to Linda and said, "You know, the best investment we ever made was hiring someone who knew what they were doing." We had not promised them extraordinary returns or secret investment strategies. Instead, he provided something far more valuable: a plan, discipline, and peace of mind.

This example is provided for illustrative purposes only and does not represent typical results. Financial outcomes vary significantly based on individual circumstances.

Story Two: When Advice Goes Wrong

Several years earlier, another retiree named Harold had walked into a different advisor's office with a similar goal of securing his retirement. Harold had spent his career as a small business owner. After selling his plumbing company at age sixty-five, he walked away with nearly $900,000 in savings. He had never been particularly comfortable with investments and hoped to find someone he could trust to manage the money.

The advisor he met seemed confident and persuasive. His office walls were covered with awards and framed certificates. He spoke enthusiastically about "high-performance opportunities" and "exclusive strategies." Harold was impressed.

During their first meeting, the advisor told Harold that traditional investments like bonds and diversified funds were outdated and produced "mediocre returns." Instead, he recommended placing a large portion of Harold's savings into a series of complex investment products that promised higher income and growth. The advisor assured him that these investments were "perfect for retirees." Trusting the professional sitting across the desk, Harold agreed.

What Harold did not fully understand were the high fees, surrender charges, and risks associated with the products he purchased. Much of his savings became locked into long-term investments that limited his flexibility. In addition, the advisor had earned significant commissions from the transactions. For the first year, Harold received the income payments he had been promised, and everything seemed fine.

Then the market changed. Several of the investments began to decline in value. Because of surrender penalties, Harold could not easily withdraw his funds or move them to safer alternatives. Meanwhile, the income payments he relied on began to shrink. When Harold tried to contact his advisor for help, the responses became increasingly vague.

"Markets fluctuate," the advisor told him during one conversation. "You just have to stay patient."

Patience did not solve Harold's problem. Over time, he realized that the investments had been designed primarily to benefit the advisor, not the client. The fees continued regardless of performance, and the complexity of the products made it difficult to unwind the strategy without significant losses. Eventually, Harold sought a second opinion from another financial professional. After reviewing the situation, the new advisor explained that many of the investments were unsuitable for someone in Harold's stage of life.

Although steps were taken to gradually repair the damage, some losses could not be recovered. The experience left Harold with a hard-earned lesson. He later told a friend, "I thought I had hired someone to protect my retirement. What I really hired was a salesperson."

This example is provided for illustrative purposes only and does not represent typical results. Financial outcomes vary significantly based on individual circumstances.

These two stories highlight an important truth.

A good financial advisor serves as a guide and fiduciary, placing the client's interests first, creating a thoughtful plan, and helping navigate complex financial decisions. A poor advisor, on the other hand, may prioritize commissions or personal gain, often leaving clients exposed to unnecessary risks and costly mistakes. Choosing the right advisor is one of the most important financial decisions anyone can make because when it comes to your retirement, the difference between good advice and bad advice can shape the rest of your life.

PLANNING IS AN ONGOING PROCESS

Financial planning is not something that happens once and is then forgotten. Markets change, families grow, health circumstances evolve, and tax laws shift. A sound financial plan should be reviewed regularly and adjusted as needed. Annual reviews with financial advisors, attorneys, and tax professionals can ensure that strategies remain aligned with current goals and changing circumstances. By treating financial planning as an ongoing process rather than a one-time event, individuals can maintain confidence that their strategies remain effective.

Perhaps the greatest obstacle to effective planning is procrastination. Many individuals postpone financial decisions because they feel overwhelmed by complexity or believe there will be more time later. Unfortunately, delaying action often leads to missed opportunities and avoidable complications. The earlier you begin planning, the greater the number of options available to you. Early planning allows for better tax strategies, more flexible investment decisions, and greater control over how assets are transferred to future generations.

Waiting too long can limit those options and create unnecessary stress for both you and your family. The best time to start planning was yesterday. The second-best time is today.

If there is one message I hope readers take from this book, it is this: do not wait. Start by taking a few simple steps:

- Organize your financial documents.
- Create or update your will.
- Review your beneficiary designations.
- Evaluate your retirement income strategy.
- Discuss your plans with your family.
- Seek professional guidance when necessary.

These steps may seem small, but together they create the foundation for long-term financial security. At the heart of financial planning is the simple idea that preparation provides freedom. When your finances are organized and your plans are in place, you gain the freedom to focus on the things that matter most to you, such as family, health, purpose, and community. You gain confidence that your retirement years will be secure. You gain the peace of mind that your loved ones will be protected, and perhaps most importantly, you gain the satisfaction of knowing that the life you have built will continue to benefit others long after you are gone.

Your legacy is not defined solely by the assets you accumulate. It is defined by the values you demonstrate, the relationships you nurture, and the positive influence you leave behind. With thoughtful planning, discipline, and the guidance of trusted professionals, you can ensure that your financial journey ends with stability, purpose, and lasting impact. The opportunity to take control of that future is in your hands.

The time to act is now.

ACKNOWLEDGMENTS

As I reflect on the journey of bringing this book to life, there are a few individuals whose support and guidance made a meaningful difference along the way.

I would like to extend my sincere gratitude to Divya Parekh and her incredible team. Your insight, encouragement, and steady guidance helped shape not only the direction of this book but also my confidence in sharing these ideas. Your professionalism and genuine care made what could have been an overwhelming process feel both manageable and rewarding.

I am also deeply thankful to Danielle Fitzpatrick-Clark for her support and influence throughout this journey. Your ability to connect, inspire, and bring clarity to the message played an important role in helping this work reach its full potential. Your encouragement meant more than you may realize.

To both of you, thank you for being part of this process and for helping turn this vision into something real. I am truly grateful.

ABOUT THE AUTHOR

In 2004, Mario founded BGS Capital Management LLC, where he serves as Managing Partner. He has been instrumental in building a highly successful wealth management practice that is nationally recognized by its broker-dealer, Cetera Financial Specialists. The firm oversees approximately $400 million in assets under management and serves over 2,000 clients.

Mario holds Series 7, Series 66, and Series 24 registrations and is licensed in more than 30 states. He also maintains licenses in Life, Health, Disability, and Casualty insurance. His professional designations include Accredited Investment Fiduciary®, Chartered Life Underwriter®, Chartered Financial Consultant®, and Chartered Leadership Fellow®. In addition, Mario holds an NMLS Mortgage License (#269691) and is a commissioned New Jersey Notary (#2389662) and certified signing agent.

BGS Capital Management has been recognized by New Jersey Monthly magazine as a Five Star Top Wealth Management firm, and Mario has been named to the Executive Council within Cetera Financial Specialists for eight consecutive years.

Mario is also the founder of BGS Assurance LLC, a learning institute that provides continuing education to insurance and mortgage professionals. A former NASBA-recognized continuing education provider, he has taught courses to CPA and tax professionals across the United States.

As a public speaker, Mario delivers engaging and motivational seminars on wealth creation for individuals, as well as insights for business owners navigating an increasingly technology-driven marketplace.

Most recently, Mario authored The Art of Creating Wealth, which has sold over 1100 copies on Amazon and is now available at Barnes & Noble.

DISCLOSURE AND DISCLAIMER

The views and opinions expressed in the content of this book are solely those of the author, Mario Sicari. The information in this book is provided for educational and informational purposes only. While reasonable efforts have been made to present accurate information, no guarantee is made regarding its completeness, accuracy, or applicability to any individual situation. All examples of mutual funds, stocks, and other securities are not intended as a solicitation. These examples are intended to be used in an educational format. The author and publisher make no attempt to recommend that any reader buy, sell, hold, or purchase any mutual fund, stock, security, insurance product, or other financial product. Should anyone consider the purchase or sale of any mutual fund, stock, security, insurance product, or other financial product, they should consult with an appropriately licensed financial professional and tax advisor.

Nothing in this book should be construed as financial, investment, legal, tax, accounting, insurance, or business advice. Readers should consult with appropriately licensed professionals before making any financial, investment, tax, legal, accounting, insurance, or business decisions.

Mario Sicari is a registered representative with Cetera Financial Specialists LLC. He is a chartered life underwriter, chartered financial consultant, accredited investment fiduciary, and a charter leadership fellow. He is a certified instructor with NASBA (National Association of Board Accountancy), offering continuing education credits to accountants and certified public accountants. He is a certified life, health, property, casualty, and annuity instructor in the State of New Jersey, offering continuing education to licensed brokers in the State of New Jersey. He is also a licensed mortgage representative in the State of New

Jersey, NMLS# 269690. FINRA CRD# 2365508.

1.) Securities offered through Cetera Financial Specialists LLC (doing insurance business in CA as CFGFS Insurance Agency LLC, CA insurance license #0E28878), member FINRA/SIPC. Advisory services offered through Cetera Investment Advisers LLC. Cetera firms are under separate ownership from any other named entity. 201 WEST PASSAIC STREET, SUITE 301, ROCHELLE PARK, NJ 07662.

2.) The views stated in this book are not necessarily the opinion of Cetera Financial Specialists LLC or Cetera Investment Advisers LLC and should not be construed directly or indirectly as an offer to buy or sell any securities mentioned herein. Due to volatility within the markets mentioned, opinions are subject to change without notice. Information is based on sources believed to be reliable; however, their accuracy or completeness cannot be guaranteed. Past performance does not guarantee future results.

3.) Neither Cetera Financial Specialists LLC nor any of its affiliates offer tax or legal services.

4.) This disclosure should be reviewed by Cetera compliance and/or legal counsel before publication to ensure it satisfies all applicable broker-dealer, advisory, securities, insurance, tax, and publishing requirements.